Fun with Maths Puzzles, Games and More

About the authors

Jamie York was born in Maine, went to state school in Connecticut, received two computer science degrees (from Rensselaer Polytechnic Institute in Troy, New York, and the University of Denver), and began teaching maths in 1985 at a boarding school in New Hampshire. In 1994, after spending two years in Nepal serving as a Peace Corps volunteer, Jamie's search for meaningful education led him to Shining Mountain Waldorf School (in Boulder, Colorado), where he is still currently teaching Middle and Upper School mathematics. Since then, he has focused largely on envisioning and creating a comprehensive and meaningful mathematics curriculum that spans Classes One to Twelve. Jamie consults at a variety of schools, teaches maths workshops, and serves on the faculty at the Center for Anthroposophy (in Wilton, New Hampshire) training Waldorf Upper School maths teachers.

Randy Evans' love affair with games started early in childhood and grew into a lifetime passion. He graduated from Duke University, North Carolina, with a BA in Philosophy in 1988 and also received a JD from the University of Denver, College of Law in 1992. He teaches Middle and Upper School maths at two Waldorf schools in Atlanta, Georgia, where he works with his wife Jenny.

Mick Follari graduated from the Green Meadow Waldorf School and went on to study Engineering at Brown University, Rhode Island. Mick is a Waldorf science and maths teacher, having taught in several schools around the US, is a web design and development consultant, and is involved in green design/build real estate projects. He lives in Boulder, Colorado.

MAKING MATHS
MEANINGFUL

Fun with Maths Puzzles, Games and More

A Resource Book for Steiner-Waldorf Teachers

Jamie York,
Mick Follari and Randy Evans

Floris
Books

First published in the United States of America
by Jamie York Press, Boulder, Colorado in 2011
www.JamieYorkPress.com
First published in the UK in 2019
by Floris Books, Edinburgh,
adapted from the 2012 American edition

British Library CIP Data available
ISBN 978-178250-568-6
Printed in Great Britain by TJ International

Contents

Introduction

The purpose of this book

This book is intended as a resource for maths teachers in Classes Four to Twelve, in part, to supplement the normal classroom material, such as the *Making Maths Meaningful* middle school workbooks.

There may be times when things seem to get dull and the students begin to lose their spark. It is then that the teacher knows it is time to do something different. This book provides ideas for that 'something different'.

What makes this book unique?

There are many maths puzzle books available today. However, it can be daunting for a teacher (especially a teacher in the lower classes for whom maths is not a specialty) to pick up a maths puzzle book that consists of a couple hundred puzzles, and find a good one that would work well for tomorrow's maths class.

This book is specifically geared toward the teacher who needs to find an excellent puzzle or game for tomorrow's class. We have tried to limit the number of puzzles and games to just a few excellent ones. We have categorised the puzzles according to class level.

Skills and thrills

Unfortunately, there is an over-emphasis today on the mastery of skills in mathematics curricula. Even for students who appear to be successful, their experience with maths amounts to a long list of procedures to be followed in order to solve problems, many of which may seem to be quite meaningless. All too often, the repetition and drill of solving endless problems from a textbook or workbook can kill the students' natural enthusiasm for learning. We believe that all students should have the opportunity to experience the *thrill of mathematics*.

What is this thrill of mathematics? It is perhaps best experienced when students encounter a challenge – often a challenge that at first seems formidable – and they persevere and emerge successful. A good maths puzzle or game provides an excellent opportunity for such a thrill.

This is not to say that skills aren't important; they are. But, it is equally important for students to experience meaningful maths, and to be enthusiastic about learning maths.

The art of teaching maths is, at least partly, how to balance all of this.

The art of problem solving

There is a difference between *solving problems* (e.g., doing a problem on a homework sheet) and *problem solving*.

Usually solving problems amounts to following procedures that the students have been previously shown how to do. Often, this aspect of maths teaching is essential and effective. However, even a typical word problem isn't genuine problem solving.

So what is *genuine problem solving?* There are shades of grey here, but true problem solving must include an experience of uncertainty. The student is likely to say to himself, 'I have never seen this before – I have no idea what to do.' Thus begins a problem-solving experience.

These kinds of problem-solving experiences may occasionally be encountered through a daily homework assignment, but usually the teacher needs to carefully

Fun With Maths Puzzles, Games and More

plan these experiences. A good puzzle or game is one way to give the students a genuine problem-solving experience.

To some degree, real problem solving should receive a greater emphasis in the later Upper School years, but there should be elements of problem solving in the earlier years as well.

Guidelines for using this book

This book is divided into the following sections:

Puzzles

There are about 50 puzzles for each class (Classes Four to Eight) and roughly 90 puzzles for the Upper School.

Looking for easier puzzles for your class? Try taking puzzles from an earlier class. For example, many of the puzzles listed as Classes Five to Eight can be quite fun for Upper School students.

In each section, the easier puzzles are generally first, and then the puzzles generally get more difficult.

It is intended that all puzzles for Classes Four to Eight should be solved without the use of algebra. With some of the Upper School puzzles, algebra may be helpful.

Carefully plan how to give a puzzle to the class. Puzzles with many steps lend themselves to working in small groups. Some puzzles that can be solved quickly by one student who 'sees' the special trick, might be discouraging for another student who doesn't 'get it'. Such puzzles can be given at the end of a homework assignment or test.

Games

The intention in this book is to have just a few excellent games for the teacher to choose from. Even for the teacher who loves playing games with his class, it may be enough to introduce just a couple of new games over the course of the year. A puzzle is a one-time experience; a good maths game can be played again and again, each time providing new benefits.

Maths magic tricks

These great attention-grabbers help to develop a sense of wonder for numbers. They are especially effective in Classes Four to Seven, but can also be used in the higher classes as an interesting algebra exercise to show why a given maths trick works. Additionally, there are around 30 tricks (for calculating quickly in your head) that are found at the back of the Class Six and Class Seven *Making Maths Meaningful* workbooks.

Classroom activities

This is a modest collection of activities that could turn out to be the highlight of the year for a maths class.

Solutions

Solutions to the puzzles are at the end of the book. Of course, it may be best for the teacher to try solving the puzzle (before looking at the solution) in order to fully experience what the students will go through.

With some puzzles, there may be several possible solutions. In those cases, the solution key usually gives only one of the possible solutions.

Acknowledgments

The authors would like to thank the following people for their contributions to this book. Sharon Annan, Claudio Salusso, Harry Kretz, Oliver Goddu, Willy Douglas, Zack Newkumet, Waleska Suarez, Marlene Kountze, Miriam Barton, Ben Alexandra, Matthew Messner, David Gresham, Kyle Brown, Mischa Samson, E.J. Alexandra, Alex Freuman, Conor Parrish, Wim Gottenbos, Nettie Fabrie, Lisa Ayrault, Max Herz, Oliver McCammon, and Andrew Starzynski.

An extra special thanks goes to Peter Taylor for providing the inspiration for much of the section problem-solving exercises in the Upper School chapter.

Class Four Puzzles

1. Coin puzzles

a) Pete has 15 coins (10p and 5p coins only) worth £0.95 in his pocket. How many of each type of coin does he have?

b) Mary has 30 coins worth £2.70 in her pocket. How many of each type of coin does she have if she has only 10p and 5p coins?

c) Mary has 30 coins worth £2.70 in her pocket. How many of each type of coin does she have if she has only 20p and 5p coins?

2. Counting squares

How many squares are there in this figure?

3. Form tracing

Trace the following form without lifting your pencil off the page or going over the same line twice. (What do you need to do to make this possible?)

4. A basket of fruit

a) Mary has a basket of cherries. If she counts them by 3s, she has 2 left over. If she counts them by 5s, she has 4 left over. How many cherries are there? (There is more than one possible answer.)

b) John has a basket of apples. If he counts them by 3s, he has 1 left over. If he counts them by 4s, he has 3 left over. How many apples are there? (There is more than one possible answer.)

5. Sums and differences
a) Find two numbers that add to 24 and subtract to 14.

b) Find two numbers that add to 24 and subtract to 2.

c) Find two numbers that add to 53 and subtract to 13.

6. Halfway between
a) What number is halfway between 15 and 21?

b) What number is halfway between 32 and 42?

c) What number is halfway between 45 and 61?

d) What number is halfway between 420 and 480?

e) What number is halfway between 740 and 770?

7. Products, sums and differences
a) Find two numbers that multiply to 36 and
    i) add to 13.   *ii)* add to 15.
    iii) add to 37.

b) Find two numbers that multiply to 24 and
    i) subtract to 10.   *ii)* subtract to 2.

c) Find two numbers that multiply to 48 and
   i) add to 14.   *ii)* add to 16.
   iii) add to 26.

d) Find two numbers that multiply to 40 and
   i) subtract to 3.   *ii)* subtract to 18.

e) Find two numbers that multiply to 100 and
   i) add to 52.   *ii)* add to 25.

8. Missing-digit arithmetic

Fill in the missing digits (indicated by ?) for these problems. (See puzzles in other classes for more problems like this.)

a)

```
    4?8
+   ?6?
   ?220
```

b)

```
     ?7
×    5?
     94
+  ???0
   ????
```

c)

```
     ?3
×    5?
    3?2
+  ??50
   ??8?
```

9. Money problems

a) Jane bought 7 apples at a price of 33p per apple. If she gave the cashier £5.31, what did the cashier give her back in change?

b) Henry earns £90 per day at his job. He works 5 days per week. He pays £150 per week for rent, and £85 per week on food. After rent and food, how much money does he have per week for everything else?

c) For her birthday party, Janet bought 3 litres of ice cream. A litre of ice cream costs £3.69. How much change did she get back if she gave the cashier £20.07?

d) Mary wants to buy a bicycle that costs £240. She has already saved £75. If, starting now, she saves £11 every month, how long will it take her to save enough money to buy the bicycle?

e) Two popsicles and one chocolate bar cost £2.10. One of each costs £1.45. What does a chocolate bar cost?

f) The amusement park charges £5.50 for an entrance fee, and then £2.50 for each ride. How many rides can Hillary do if she starts out with £20?

g) Stacey rides the bus every day back and forth from her house to her work. How much did she have to pay for riding the bus last month, if she worked 18 days, and the cost to ride the bus is £1.40 per one-way trip?

h) If Peter eats at his favourite restaurant twice per week, and it costs him £14 each time, how much will it cost him over the course of a year?

i) Jenny and Taylor went to dinner and split the cost, but not evenly. The total cost for the dinner was £28. How much did Jenny pay if she paid £5 less than Taylor?

j) Maria has already saved £70. How many more weeks will it take her to save a total of £310, if she saves an additional £30 per week?

k) Gary has twice as much money as Bob, and Kate has £6 less than Gary. How much do the three of them have combined, if Kate has £18?

10. Measurement problems

a) If a tree grows 3½ cm every month, how tall (in metres) will it be when it is 50 years old?

b) Paul has 4 pieces of string with a total combined length of exactly 60 cm. Three of the pieces are the same length, and one piece is 24 cm long. How long are the other pieces?

c) A board that is 6 metres long is cut into 16 equally long pieces. How long is each piece?

d) A brick wall was made with a total of 5000 bricks. If each brick weighs 3½ kg, how many tonnes do all of the bricks weigh together?

11. Measuring a brick

A brick is twice as long as it is wide.

a) How wide is the brick if it is 22½ cm long?

b) How wide is the brick if it is 21½ cm long?

c) How long is the brick if it is 10¾ cm wide?

d) If one brick is 22½ cm long, how long would 20 bricks be that are placed end-to-end?

12. Counting problems

a) Ross has 127 marbles and Jeffrey has 213 marbles. How many marbles does Jeffrey need to give Ross so that both boys end up with the same number of marbles?

b) Mary has 3 more apples than Ted and 3 times as many apples as Alex. How many apples do they have combined if Mary has 24 apples?

c) Jane and John started with a total of 30 biscuits between them. John then ate 3 of his biscuits, which left him with exactly twice as many biscuits as Jane. How many biscuits did Jane have?

d) Lori is on the middle step of a staircase. She goes down 3 steps, up 6 steps, then down 11 steps. She is now on the bottom step of the staircase. How many steps does the staircase have?

13. Favourite numbers

a) If Jill subtracts 7 from her favourite number, multiplies by 10, and adds 7, the result is 47. What is her favourite number?

b) If Christine takes her favourite number, subtracts 6, and multiplies by 5, she ends up with 35. What is Christine's favourite number?

c) If Billy doubles his favourite number and subtracts 5, he ends up with 57. What is his favourite number?

d) If George divides his favourite number by 3 and multiplies it by 5, he gets 85. What is his favourite number?

e) If Jack adds 16 to his favourite number, cuts it in half, divides by 5, and subtracts 2, the result is 1. What is his favourite number?

f) If Lucy takes her favourite number, multiplies it times itself, subtracts 4, divides by 12, adds 6, and multiplies by 7, she ends up with 77. What is Lucy's favourite number?

g) If Lexie takes her favourite number, adds 5, divides by 6, subtracts 7, multiplies by 73, and adds 8, she ends up with 8. What is Lexie's favourite number?

14. Lots of pets

a) Iris has twice as many pets as Lizzy. Lizzy, Naomi, and Iris have a total of 14 pets between them. If Iris has 6 pets, how many pets does Naomi have?

b) Mark has twice as many pets as Jen. If they have 15 pets together, how many pets does Jen have?

c) Amy has 3 more pets than Catherine, and Beth has 5 more pets than Amy. How many pets do the three girls have all together if Beth has 11 pets?

Class Five Puzzles

15. Pets' legs

All of Jane's pets are either cats or birds. How many cats and birds does Jane have
a) if she has 3 pets and they have a total of 10 legs?
b) if she has 10 pets and they have a total of 32 legs?

16. In the middle

John is both the tenth tallest and the tenth shortest in his class. How many students are in his class?

17. Filling in the boxes

Put each of the digits 1, 2, 3, 4, 5, 6 into a box in order to create a correct multiplication problem.

18. Triangle flipping

How can you move only three of the coins and end up with the same triangle, but upside down?

19. Counting triangles

How many triangles are there in this figure?

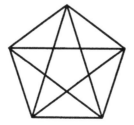

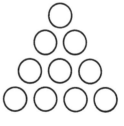

20. A cricket ball and a bat

Kate bought a cricket ball and a bat for £110. How much did the cricket ball cost if the bat cost £100 more than the cricket ball?

21. Five odd numbers

Find five consecutive odd numbers that add to 155.

22. Enough children

What is the least number of children someone could have such that every child would have at least two brothers and at least two sisters?

23. Counting racers

a) The organiser of a race notices that if she divides the total number of racers into groups of four, there are two left over, and if she divides them into groups of three, there is one left over. How many racers are there? (There is more than one possible answer.)

b) The organiser of a race notices that if she divides the total number of racers into groups of four, there are three left over, and if she divides them into groups of five, there are three left over. How many racers are there? (There is more than one possible answer.)

24. My favourite number

My favourite number is 142,857. Calculate the following in order to find out why it is my favourite number. Look for patterns!

a) Find twice my favourite number.

b) Find three times my favourite number.

c) Find four times my favourite number.

d) Find five times my favourite number.

e) Find six times my favourite number.

f) Find seven times my favourite number.

25. A clock riddle

a) Cathy said to her friend, 'Fifteen minutes ago, it was twice as many minutes after 4 o'clock as it is now before 5 o'clock.' What time was it when Cathy said that?

b) Andrew said to his friend, 'Half an hour ago, it was four times as many minutes after 7 o'clock as it is now before 8 o'clock.' What time was it when Andrew said that?

26. A 4 × 4 magic square

Fill in the rest of the empty boxes of the magic square such that each row, column, and diagonal have a magic sum equal to 50. Also, the four corners, and the middle four cells should add to 50.

7			12
	8	23	5
9	16		

27. Sums and differences

a) Find two numbers that add to 50 and subtract to 12.

b) Find two numbers that add to 50 and subtract to 36.

c) Find two numbers that add to 89 and subtract to 15.

28. Halfway between

a) What number is halfway between 13 and 16?

b) What number is halfway between 32 and 50?

c) What number is halfway between 378 and 400?

d) What number is halfway between 3,000,000 and 6,000,000?

29. Amicable numbers

Note: This problem deals with amicable numbers and could serve as an excellent challenge problem for Class 5 students during a 'Wonder of Numbers' main lesson.

 With each of the two numbers 220 and 284, add together all of its factors (except for itself). What do you notice?

30. Coin puzzles

a) Frank has 24 coins (20p and 5p coins only) worth £3.45 in his pocket. How many of each type of coin does he have?

b) Courtney has 29 coins (10p and 20p coins only) worth £5.00 in her pocket. How many of each type of coin does she have?

31. Products, sums and differences

a) Find three consecutive whole numbers that have a product of 60.

b) Find two numbers that multiply to 30 and
  i) add to 13.
  ii) add to 11.
  iii) add to 17.

  iv) subtract to 1.
  v) subtract to 13.

c) Find two numbers that multiply to 60 and

  i) add to 16.

  ii) add to 17.

  iii) subtract to 17.

  iv) add to 23.

  v) subtract to 28.

32. Sums of primes

Note: In order to do these problems, the students need a list (ideally one that they have created) of all the prime numbers less than 100.

a) Find two prime numbers that add to 36 (there are four different solutions).

b) Find two prime numbers that add to 90 (there are nine different solutions).

c) Find three prime numbers that add to 35. (*Hint:* two of the numbers may be the same. There are eight different solutions.)

33. Age puzzles

a) Jeff is half as old as Pete. Next year, their ages will add to 35. How old is Jeff?

b) Hannah is 8 and her father is 30. How long will it be until Hannah is half her father's age?

c) If Sarah takes her age, divides it by 3, adds 6, and lastly multiples by 2, she ends up with 22. How old is Sarah?

d) Next year, Jimmy will be double Betty's age. How old will Jimmy be in 10 years, if Betty is 7 now?

34. Money problems

a) At the local store bananas cost 76p per kg, and oranges cost 24p each. If Mark buys 3 kg of bananas and 8 oranges, how much change will he get back if he gives the cashier £10.20.

b) How many weeks will it take Jordan to save a total of £500, if he saves £30 per week, and if he has already saved £115?

c) Jason bought 4 morning rolls and 2 litres of milk at the local shop. His total bill was for £2.42. If the milk cost £1.38, how much does one roll cost?

d) If petrol costs £1.38 per litre, and Grace buys 35 litres, how much change will she get back if she gives the cashier a £50 note?

35. Missing-digit arithmetic

Fill in the missing digits (indicated by ?) for these problems. (See puzzles in other classes for more problems like this.)

a)	*b)*	*c)*	*d)*
$\begin{array}{r} 34? \\ +\ \ ??5 \\ \hline ?153 \end{array}$	$\begin{array}{r} ?3 \\ \times\ \ 5? \\ \hline ??1 \\ +\ \ 41?0 \\ \hline ???? \end{array}$	$\begin{array}{r} 7? \\ \times\ \ ?5 \\ \hline ?90 \\ +\ ??20 \\ \hline ?5?? \end{array}$	$\begin{array}{r} ??7 \\ \times\ \ 3?? \\ \hline ?0?3 \\ ?1?0 \\ +\ ?5?00 \\ \hline ?7??? \end{array}$

36. Fraction problems

a) A board is cut into three pieces. If the pieces have lengths of $25\frac{1}{2}$ cm, $39\frac{3}{4}$ cm, and $120\frac{3}{4}$ cm, how long was the original piece before it was cut?

b) A board is 190 cm long. Three pieces, each $53\frac{7}{8}$ cm long, are cut off the board. How long is the piece that is left over?

37. Measurement problems

a) Lisa is having a party for 73 guests. She figures that, on average, each person will drink a glass of juice. The glasses hold 175 mℓ. How many litres of juice does she need to buy for her party?

b) The total weight of 6 identical plums and 8 identical oranges is exactly $2\frac{1}{4}$ kg. If each plum weighs 115 g, how much does each orange weigh?

c) Jen owns an apple orchard. Yesterday, her farm harvested 42,000 apples. If each apple weighs 140 g on average, what is the total weight of the apples, and how many boxes are needed if each box holds 30 kg?

d) At Bob's shop, a packet of 4 peaches cost £1.49, and at Fred's shop the same size peaches cost £1.16 for a packet of 3. What is the cost of each peach in Bob's shop, and are they cheaper than at Fred's?

38. Lots of pets

a) Sam has 3 fewer pets than Nancy. Emily has as many pets as Sam and Nancy combined. If Nancy has twice as many pets as Sam, how many pets does Emily have?

b) Kate has two more pets than Jessica, and Abby has two more pets than Kate. If Kate had one more pet, then she would have twice as many pets as Jessica. How many pets does Abby have?

c) Jake and Franny have 7 pets between the two of them. Steve has twice as many pets as Jake. Steve has 5 more pets than Franny. How many pets do the three children have all together?

39. Unit cost and proportions

a) If 10 kg of bananas cost £7.60, how much do 8 kg of bananas cost?

b) If 3 boxes of cereal cost £4.92, how much do 7 boxes of cereal cost?

c) If 4.6 kg of potatoes cost £3.68, how much would 7.6 kg of potatoes cost?

d) At John's favourite amusement park, you pay for a go-cart ride by the minute. If a 30-minute ride costs £4.50, what is the cost of a 35-minute ride?

e) If it takes Kate 3 hours to bike 72 km, how long would it take her to bike 96 km?

f) If it takes Edward 15 minutes to type 540 words, how long would it take him to type 900 words?

g) If it takes Ken 2 hours and 15 minutes to drive 180 km, how long would it take him to drive 380 km?

40. Counting problems

a) Lexie has two-thirds as much money as Fiona, and Sam has £8 less than Fiona. How much do the three of them have combined if Sam has £10?

b) William and Beth have £25 combined. If Beth gives £6 to William, then William will have £3 more than Beth. How much money did Beth have in the beginning?

c) Two-thirds of the students in Mr Smith's class are girls. If there are 12 boys in the class, how many total students are there in the class?

d) Kevin has 5 more marbles than Fred. Rex has 14 fewer marbles than Kevin and Fred combined. How many marbles do the boys have altogether, if Rex has 15 marbles?

e) Suzy has 6 more cards than Ann. If Ann gives 2 cards to Suzy, then Suzy will have 3 times as many cards as Ann. How many cards did they both start out with?

f) Frank and Dexter together made 24 Christmas cards. Frank made one-third as many as Dexter. How many cards did Frank make?

Class Six Puzzles

Note: Some of the puzzles in this section could be solved by using algebra. The intention, however, is to solve them without the use of algebra. In this way, the process is likely to be less mechanical and will allow the students to enter more fully into a pure problem-solving experience.

41. Trading cats
A boy said to a girl, 'Give me one of your cats and I'll have as many cats as you have.' The girl then replied, 'True, but if you give me one of your cats, I'll have twice as many as you.' How many cats did they each have to begin with?

42. Trading cards
Keith has twice as many cards as Ben. If Keith gives 10 cards to Ben, then Ben will have 3 times as many cards as Keith. How many cards did they both start out with?

43. Comparing money
Ron has £4 more than half as much as Tim. Paula has ¾ as much as Ron. How much do the three of them have combined, if Paula has £24?

44. Weighing coins
One 20p coin weighs 5 grams. How many kg does £100 in 20p coins weigh?

45. Cutting a board
How long does it take to cut a 240 cm board into 12 20-cm pieces, if each cut takes 30 seconds?

46. Summing primes

a) Find three prime numbers that have a sum of 41.

b) Find four prime numbers that have a sum of 41.

47. The chicken, the fox, and the sack of grain

Jeff must carry a chicken, a fox, and a sack of grain across a bridge. However, he can only carry one at a time, and he cannot leave the chicken alone with the grain or leave the fox alone with the chicken. How can he do this?

48. The hungry cat

A cat ate 100 mice in 5 days. On each day (except the first) he ate 3 more mice than he did the day before. How many mice did he eat on the first day?

49. Counting siblings

Each of my daughters has as many sisters as brothers, but each of my sons has twice as many sisters as brothers. How many sons and daughters do I have?

50. Giving change

George asked for change for a pound and he received 15 coins. How was this done?

51. Football games

Here are some facts about Premier League football:

There are 20 teams.

Each team plays 38 matches in a season.

In every game there is one match ball, but to keep things moving there are 16 balls at each match.

The weight of a football is between 410 g and 450 g.

a) How many Premier League matches are played every season?

b) How many footballs in total are used in Premier League matches every season?

c) If all of those footballs were gathered together, what would the total weight be, assuming an average weight? (Give your answer in kg to 2 significant figures.)

52. Stick puzzles
With each puzzle, every stick must be part of a square. No two sticks may be placed on top of each other or side by side.

a) Move two sticks so that you end up with exactly two squares.

b) Move four sticks to make exactly three squares.

c) Move two sticks into a new position, so that you end up with exactly four squares.

d) This is a glass with a ball in it. Move two sticks so that the glass ends up upside down, and the ball is *not* inside the glass.

53. Number wheel
Use the numbers 1 through 11 to fill in each circle. Arrange it so that for any three circles which fall on a straight line, the sum of the three numbers will always be the same.

Extra challenge: which numbers can possibly be in the middle?

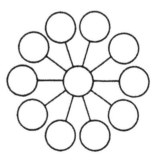

54. Cutting cake
How can a cake be cut into eight pieces by making only three straight cuts with a (normal) knife?

55. Counting marbles
If Jake counts his marbles in groups of 7, he has 3 left over. If he counts them by 4's, he has 1 left over. How many marbles are there? (There is more than one possible answer.)

56. Cutting pizza
John cut a square pizza into three pieces by first cutting the pizza into two equal-sized rectangles, then cutting one of the rectangles into two squares. He then gave a small (square) piece to each of his two brothers and kept the large piece for himself. How should he then cut two small pieces off the large rectangular piece, so that he can give these small pieces to his brothers, and everyone will end up with an equal amount of pizza?

57. Arranging letters
Place four *A*'s, four *B*'s, four *C*'s and four *D*'s into the grid such that no two of the same letter appear in the same line, horizontally or vertically, nor along the two main diagonals. You must start with *A, B, C, D* on the top row.

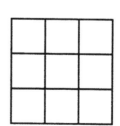

58. A 3 × 3 magic square
Use the numbers 1 through 9 only once and fill in the grid shown on the right, so that each row, column and diagonal has the same sum. (See more regarding magic squares in the 'Classroom Activities' chapter.)

59. Dartboard
John's dartboard has scores of 16, 17, 23, 24. How can someone get a score of exactly 100?

60. Form tracing
Trace the following form without lifting your pencil off the page, retracing any part of the form, or crossing through any line you've already traced.

61. A string of digits
Using the string of digits below, place plus and minus signs between some of the digits such that the result is 100. For example, we could do 9 + 87 – 65 – 4 + 321, but that gives us 348 instead the desired outcome of 100.

   9 8 7 6 5 4 3 2 1

62. Sums and differences
a) Find two numbers that add to 41 and subtract to 7.

b) Find two numbers that add to 496 and subtract to 132.

63. Halfway between
a) What number is halfway between 63 and 68?

b) What number is halfway between 630 and 680?

c) What number is halfway between 63,000 and 68,000?

d) What number is halfway between 5.3 and 5.9?

Fun With Maths Puzzles, Games and More

e) What number is halfway between 7.2 and 7.5?

f) What number is halfway between 9 and 9¼?

g) What number is halfway between 7½ and 7¾?

h) What number is halfway between 5½ and 5⅓?

64. Products, sums and differences
a) Find two numbers that multiply to 40 and
    i) add to 13.   *iii)* add to 22.
    ii) add to 14.

b) Find two numbers that multiply to 240 and
    i) add to 38.   *iv)* add to 34.
    ii) add to 83.   *v)* subtract to 34.
    iii) subtract to 1.   *vi)* add to 53.

c) Find two numbers whose product is 432 and sum is 62.

d) Find two numbers whose product is 682 and sum is 73.

65. Cricket score
In a school cricket game, Tumingham beat Ambleton by 18 runs. Twice Tumingham's runs were 6 less than 3 times Ambleton's runs. What were Tumingham's runs?

66. Fraction problems
a) A brick is 22½ cm long and 11¼ cm wide. A rectangular patio is made by placing bricks next to one another in 50 rows and 50 columns. What are the dimensions (length and width) of this patio?

b) Lori plans to make two chairs, where each leg is 39¼ cm long. The legs are all cut from a 5 by 5 cm piece of wood, and this wood is sold in lengths of 2.4, 3, 3.6, 4.2 and 4.8 metres. If Lori wants to buy only one (5 by 5 cm) piece of wood, how long should it be?

67. Coin puzzles
a) Kate has a pocketful of 20p and 50p coins. How many 50p coins are there if there are a total of 29 coins and they are worth £9.70?

b) Jeff has 50 coins worth £6.80 in his pocket. If he has only 20p and 10p coins, how many of each type of coin does he have?

68. Age puzzles
a) Bill is two-thirds of Mark's age. If Mark is 5 years older than Bill, how old is Bill?

b) Jeff is 17 years older than Sue. In 11 years, Jeff will be twice as old as Sue. How old are they both now?

c) Tim's and Wendy's ages add to 30 years. Three years ago, Tim was three times as old as Wendy. How old is Tim now?

d) The ages of Joan's children are 4, 7, 9, and 12. The sum of the ages of her daughters is 20 years. How many sisters does Joan's youngest child have?

69. Digit arithmetic puzzles

With each of the following puzzles, you must put in a digit for each letter. The same digit must be put into the same letters, and different letters must have different digits. (See puzzles in other classes for more problems like this.)

a)
```
      M
      M
  +   M
  ─────
     NM
```

b)
```
     PQ
  +   Q
  ─────
     QP
```

c)
```
   ABCD
     CD
  + EFGH
  ──────
   IJDH
```

70. Missing-digit multiplication

Fill in the missing digits (indicated by '?') for these problems. (See puzzles in other classes for more problems like this.)

a)
```
      ???
   ×   74
   ──────
     2152
  + ????0
  ───────
    ?????
```

b)
```
       ?9
    ×  ??
    ─────
      ?77
  +  4??0
  ───────
     ?30?
```

c)
```
     ?3??
   ×   ??
   ──────
     4?72
  + ???20
  ───────
    ?2??2
```

Class Seven Puzzles

Note: Some of the puzzles in this section could be solved by using algebra. The intention, however, is to solve them without the use of algebra. In this way, the process is likely to be less mechanical and will allow the students to enter more fully into a pure problem-solving experience.

71. Building chairs
If 3 boys can build 3 chairs in 3 days, how long (at that same rate) does it take 12 boys to build 12 chairs?

72. Connected circles
Put the numbers 1 to 8 into the circles such that no two consecutive numbers are connected. For example, if we choose to put 3 into the topmost circle, then we cannot put 2 or 4 into any of the three circles just below it.

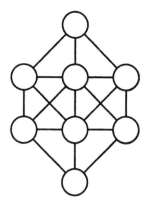

73. Hand washing
Hank's mother tells him that she will pay him £60 per hour to wash his hands. How much money does he get if it takes him 6 seconds to wash his hands?

74. A special number
An eleven-digit number is such that the first digit is 4, the last digit is 7, and the sum of any three consecutive digits is 14. Find the number.

75. Four congruent pieces

The figure shown here is as it appears to be – a square with a quarter of it missing. How can it be cut into four congruent pieces?

76. A generous king

There are 12 people standing in line to receive their gift from the king. The king gives the first person one gold coin and the second person 2 gold coins. The third person has 3 times as much as the second; the fourth person has 4 times as much as the third; the fifth person has 5 times as much as the fourth, and so on. How many gold coins does the last (twelfth) person get?

77. Connect-the-dots square

Without lifting your pencil off the page, draw four straight lines such that each of the nine dots has a line passing through it. You may not retrace a portion of a line.

78. Siblings

a) Mrs Harrison has five daughters. Each of these daughters has two brothers. How many children does Mrs Harrison have?

b) Ian and Sarah are siblings. Ian has twice as many sisters as brothers, and Sarah has twice as many brothers as sisters. How many children are in the family?

79. Stick puzzles

With each puzzle, every stick must be part of a square. No two sticks may be placed side by side.

a) Move three sticks so that you end up with exactly five squares.

b) Move three sticks so that you end up with exactly four squares.

c) Move three sticks so that you end up with exactly three squares.

d) Move two sticks so that you end up with exactly seven squares.

80. Sharing oranges
Sara has 15 oranges, Bill has 9 oranges, and Stan has none. The oranges are divided equally between the three people, and then Stan is to pay £2.80 for his share. How can the £2.80 be divided fairly between Bill and Sara?

81. Age puzzles
a) The sum of Frank's and Tim's ages is 20. Frank is a year younger than twice Tim's age. How old are they?

b) Mike is 4 years older than twice Jim's age, and 4 years younger than 3 times Jim's age. How old are they?

c) Charlotte is two-thirds of Brianna's age. Fifteen years ago Brianna was twice Charlotte's age. How old are they now?

d) Annie is 8 years older than Ben. Ben is 1 year older than Annie was when she was 3 times older than Ben. How old is Annie now?

e) Christine is 7 years younger than twice as old as Karen. Karen is 6 years younger than Christine was when she (Christine) was 3 times as old as Karen. How old are they now?

82. Mixing apple juice and milk

There are two jugs – one with a litre of apple juice, and the other with a litre of milk. Mary takes one 250 ml cup of apple juice from the apple juice pitcher, adds it to the pitcher of milk, and mixes it. Then she pours one 250 ml cup of the liquid from the mixed pitcher into the pitcher of apple juice. In the end, is there more milk in the apple juice, or more apple juice in the milk?

83. Products, sums and differences

Find two numbers that multiply to 210 and

a) add to 37.

c) add to 29.

b) subtract to 37.

d) subtract to 29.

84. Number riddles

a) Find two numbers such that their sum is 210 and their difference is 40.

b) What are the only numbers that are composite (not prime), less than 100, and are not a multiple of 2, 3 or 5?

c) Find two odd consecutive integers such that their sum is 48.

d) Twice a smaller number is 5 less than a larger number, and their difference is 11. What are the two numbers?

e) One number is 3 more than another. Four times the smaller number is 7 more than 3 times the greater. Find the two numbers.

85. Coin puzzles
a) Bob has a handful of 5p and 10p coins worth £2.45. How many 10p coins are there if there are 4 more 5p than 10p coins?

b) Maria has 40 coins worth £9.60. How many of each type of coin are there if
   i) she has only 50p and 10p coins?
   ii) she has 50p, 20p, and 10p coins, and there are an equal number of 50p and 10p coins?
   iii) she has 50p, 20p and 10p coins, and there are 2½ times as many 10p as 20p coins?

86. Digit arithmetic puzzles
With each of the following puzzles, you must put in a digit for each letter. For each problem, the same digit must be put into the same letters, and different letters must have different digits. (See puzzles in other classes for more problems like this.)

a)
```
    AB
    AB
    AB
 +  AB
    CA
```

b)
```
    ABCD
 +  EFGB
    EFCBH
```

c)
```
    ABCDB
 -  EFBGA
    HIBA
```

87. Missing-digit multiplication and division
Fill in the missing digits (indicated by ?) for these problems.

a)
```
        ??
    ? ┌─────
    ? │ ???
      -14
       2?
      -?1
        0
```

b)
```
         ??
    5? ┌──────
       │ 1???
        -?5?
         ???
        -400
           0
```

c)
```
        ??3
    ×   2??
       ?1?7
       ?7?0
  +  ?14?00
     ?25???
```

88. A long line

There are 200 people standing along a long, perfectly straight road. The first two people are 1 metre apart; the second and third are 2 metres apart; the third and fourth are 3 metres apart, and so on. How far is the last (200th) person from the first?

89. Pieces on a chessboard

Draw a standard 8 × 8 grid (as shown here) on a separate piece of paper, or find a floor with square tiles. Select eight of the squares on which to place an X (or a coin). You must do this such that no two X's lie along the same horizontal, vertical, or any of the 45° diagonal lines (not just the two main diagonals).

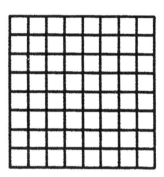

90. Chessboard squares

How many total squares are there on a chessboard? Keep in mind that a chessboard is 8 by 8, which means that it has 64 small (1 by 1) squares. But there are also squares that are 2 by 2, 3 by 3, 4 by 4, etc. (One of the 4 by 4 squares is shown here.)

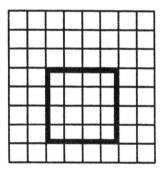

91. The race

A race was held between Abe, Ben, Charles, Dan and Ed. Find the order in which they finished, given: Dan finished two places below Ed; Ben finished one place below Charles; and Abe finished in the top three. There were no ties.

92. Two jugs

You have two jugs – one with a capacity of four litres and one with a capacity of nine litres – and you have plenty of water. There are no marks on the jugs (indicating 1 litre, 2 litres, etc.), and you may not put a mark on a jug. You may only use these two jugs.

   How can you get 1 litre into one of the jugs? How can you get 2 litres in a jug? 3 litres in a jug? 5 litres in a jug? 6 litres in a jug? 7 litres in a jug? 8 litres in a jug? (It may be best to do the easiest ones first.)

93. More pets

Alex, Ben, Charlie, and Dan each have a lot of pets. Alex has 4 fewer pets than Charlie. Ben has 3 fewer pets than Alex. Charlie has one more pet than Dan. Ben and Charlie have 15 pets between them. How many pets do the four boys have in total?

94. Concert tickets

Tickets at a concert cost £8 for section A and £4.25 for section B. In total, 4500 tickets were sold, worth £30,000. How many of each type of tickets were sold?

95. The money wizard

Peggy takes all of her money to the Money Wizard. The Money Wizard doubles her money, but then charges her a £6 fee. Peggy then takes the resulting amount of money and returns the next day to the Money Wizard. Her money is once again doubled, and then she pays the £6 fee. The same thing happens on the third day – her money is doubled and then she pays the £6 fee – but then she is left with nothing. How much money did she start with?

96. Wishful banking

You put 25p into a (very generous) bank account that doubles your money every month. How much money do you have after one year? After two years? After five years?

97. Tear and stack

Take an infinitely large sheet of paper, tear it in half, stack the two pieces, tear that stack in half, and stack the two halves on top of one another again. Continue doing this until you have torn and stacked 42 times. Estimate how high the stack will be?

98. A row of houses

Each person is a different nationality, lives in a different coloured house, drinks something different, eats something different, and has a different pet. There are no tricks.

The facts
1. There are five houses in a row.
2. The English person lives in a red house.
3. The Spaniard has a dog.
4. The person who lives in the green house drinks coffee.
5. The Ukrainian drinks tea.
6. The green house is just to the right of the ivory house.
7. The person who eats tofu has a snail.
8. Oats are eaten in the yellow house.
9. The person in the middle house drinks milk.
10. The South African lives in the house furthest to the left.
11. The pizza eater lives next to the house with a fox.
12. The person who eats oats lives next to the house with a horse.
13. The fish eater drinks orange juice.
14. The Nepali eats donuts.
15. The South African lives next to the blue house.

The questions
a) Which person drinks water?
b) Which person has a zebra?

99. Towers of Hanoi

There are three pegs (poles) and a stack of disks with holes placed on one of the pegs. The largest disk is on the bottom of the stack; the smallest is on the top. How many moves does it take to transfer the whole stack to another peg if you can only move one disk at a time, and you cannot place a larger disk on top of a smaller disk?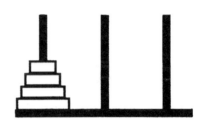

Answer this question first for a stack of 3 disks, then for a stack of 4 disks, then 5 disks, and so on.

Finally, answer the classic question: About how long does it take to move a stack of 64 disks to another peg if each move takes 1 second?

Class Eight Puzzles

Note: Some of the puzzles in this section could be solved by using algebra. The intention, however, is to solve them without the use of algebra. In this way, the process is likely to be less mechanical and will allow the students to enter more fully into a pure problem-solving experience.

100. Siblings
John and Emily are siblings. John has 5 times as many sisters as brothers, and Emily has 3 times as many sisters as brothers. How many children are in the family?

101. Socks in the dark
A dresser is filled with many white, black, green and red socks. If it is dark so you cannot see, how many single socks do you need to pull out in order to guarantee

a) that you get one pair of matching socks?

b) that you get two pairs of matching socks?

c) that you get three pairs of matching socks?

102. Brick laying
Identical bricks are laid to form a small patio as shown. Find the dimensions of a single brick if the whole patio has an area of 9450 square cm.

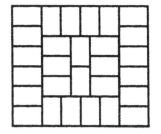

103. Jill's bike ride

Jill went on a bike ride from Brownsville to Manson passing through Gilpin along the way. After 40 minutes, she saw a sign that read, *It is half as far from here to Brownsville as it is from here to Gilpin.*

A further 36 km along the route, she had finished all but ⅕ of her trip, and it was there that she saw another sign, this time reading, *It is half as far from here to Manson as it is from here to Gilpin.*

How far is it from Brownsville to Manson? (Assume that her speed is constant.)

104. Divisibility and powers

Without calculating each power, determine if it is evenly divisible by the given number.

a) Is 19^{24} evenly divisible by 3?

b) Is 77^{31} evenly divisible by 121?

c) Is 36^{29} evenly divisible by 7?

d) Is 24^{35} evenly divisible by 5?

e) Is 35^{24} evenly divisible by 25?

f) Is 714^3 evenly divisible by 8?

g) Is 714^3 evenly divisible by 16?

h) Is $61{,}782^3$ evenly divisible by 9?

i) Is $61{,}782^3$ evenly divisible by 81?

105. Kate's grandfather

In 1981, Kate's grandfather, who was born on New Year's Day, said, 'Once, when I was younger, my age was the square root of the year.' How old was he in 1981?

106. Stick puzzles

With each puzzle, every stick must be part of a square. No two sticks may be placed side by side.

a) Move four sticks so that you end up with exactly five squares.

b) Use 11 sticks to make 11 squares.

c) Use 8 sticks to make 14 squares.

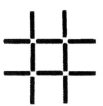

107. Digit arithmetic puzzles

With each of the following puzzles, you must put in a digit for each letter. For each problem, the same digit must be put into the same letters, and different letters must have different digits. (See puzzles in other classes for more problems like this.)

a)
```
  ABCD
+ ABBD
------
  BBAD
```

b)
```
  ABCB
- CCC
------
   CA
```

c)
```
  ABC
+ DEF
------
 GHIJ
```

108. Three schools

The sum of the number of students at Alex's school, Bob's school and Chris's school is 531. One-quarter the number of students at Bob's school is equal to half the number of students at Alex's school, and also equal to one-third the number of students at Chris's school. How many students are there at each school?

109. Arranging points

How can ten points be arranged on a page such that five straight lines can be drawn, with each line having four points on it?

110. Coin puzzles
Mark has 30 coins worth £7.80. How many of each type of coin are there if
a) there are only 20p and 50p coins?   *b)* there are only 10p and 50p coins?

c) there are 50p, 20p, and 10p coins, and there are 50% more 10p than 20p coins?

d) there are 50p, 20p, and 10p coins, and the number of 10p coins is one less than four times the number of 20p coins?

111. Tennis club
If all eight members of a tennis club played today, how long would it be before they all played on the same day again, given that:
— the first member plays every day?
— the second member plays every two days?
— the third member plays every three days?
— the fourth member plays every four days?
— the fifth member plays every five days?
— the sixth member plays every six days?
— the seventh member plays every seven days?
— the eighth member plays every eight days?

112. Number riddles
a) Find two consecutive integers such that 4 times the smaller is 4 more than 3 times the larger.

b) Find two numbers such that their product is 80 and one number is one more than 3 times the other.

c) Together a coffee and a croissant cost £3.35. The croissant costs 40p less than twice the price of the coffee. Find the price of the croissant.

d) Fran has £2 less than twice as much money as Mary. How much does Mary have if they have £41.50 together?

e) Twice Bill's weight is 12 kg less than Frank's weight, but 3 times Bill's weight is 3 kg more than Frank's weight. Find Frank's weight.

f) One number is one less than twice another number. Twice the sum of the numbers is 49. Find the two numbers.

g) The sum of two numbers is 32. The larger is 12 greater than twice the smaller. Find the numbers.

h) The difference between two numbers is 11, and the sum of their squares is 673. Find the two numbers.

113. Age puzzles

a) Cathy is 10 years older than twice Ben's age. In two years, she will be 3 times his age. How old is Cathy now?

b) The sum of Andy's and Fred's ages is 22 years. Seven years ago, Andy was 3 times Fred's age. How old are they both now?

c) Bill's age is a year less than twice Jane's age. Five years ago, Bill's age was 3 times Jane's age. Find Bill's age.

d) Karen is two-thirds as old as Bill. Three years ago, the product of their ages was 273. How old is Karen now?

e) The product of Stacy's, Tracy's and Lacy's ages is 240. Two years ago, Stacy was twice Lacy's age. How old are they now? (Give all possible answers.)

114. Shovelling snow

It takes Kate 20 minutes to shovel a square measuring 10 m by 10 m. At that rate, how long will it take her

a) to shovel a parking lot measuring 20 m by 20 m?

b) to shovel a lot measuring 100 m by 100 m?

115. Missing-digit multiplication and division

Fill in the missing digits (indicated by ?) for these problems. (See puzzles in other classes for more problems like this.)

a)

```
      ??3
  ×  ??3
      3??
     ?3?0
  + ??300
    ?????
```

b)

```
      ???7?
  ×   ?7?
      ?????
    ???2?0
  + 8?5?00
    ???5??
```

c)

```
            ??8??
  ?? |???????
      -???
        ??
       -??
        ???
       -???
          0
```

116. Six 6s

Create expressions using six 6s that equal each of the numbers from 1 to 10. For example, we could do $(666 - 66) \div 6$, but that would equal 100. Instead we want the resulting number to be something from 1 to 10.

117. Eight 8s

How can you make eight 8s equal 1000? For example, we could do $(888) \div (88 - 8) + 8 \times 8$, but that would equal 75.1. Instead, it needs to equal 1000.

118. Plane tickets

On a given flight, an airline offers two types of seats: first class for £500 and economy for £300. A total of 110 tickets were sold for £38,400. How many first class seats were sold?

119. A batch of biscuits

Sara baked a batch of biscuits. She gave one-quarter of the batch to Kevin, one-fifth to Katie, and one-sixth to Mike. If those three were given a total of 74 biscuits, how many biscuits were in the original batch?

120. Connect-the-dot squares

On the four-by-four grid shown on the right, connect four of the dots to make a square. How many possible squares are there?

121. A changing choir

A choir has 29 women and 21 men. How many women need to join the choir so that it becomes 72% women? (Assume that the number of men stays the same.)

122. The locker puzzle

Lockers in a row are numbered 1 to 300. To begin with, all of the lockers are closed, until someone comes by and opens each one. Then someone else closes every other locker, starting with locker No. 2. Another person then walks by and 'changes the state' (i.e., closes a locker if it is open or opens a locker if it is closed) of every third locker, starting with locker No. 3. Then another person changes the state of every fourth locker, starting with No. 4, etc. This process continues until a final person changes the state of only locker No. 300. The question is: which lockers are left open at the end of the whole process? You should also give an explanation for your result.

123. Shaking hands

At a convention, every person shakes hands once with every other person. If there were a total of 120 handshakes, how many people must there have been?

124. Inner tube inversion

In your imagination picture an inner tube. If you cut out a relatively small hole in the inner tube, reach through the hole with your fingers, and pull the entire inner tube through that hole, what shape do you get?

125. Slicing a triangle

Show how an equilateral triangle can be divided into 4 congruent triangles. Now show how an equilateral triangle can be divided into 6 congruent triangles. What other number of congruent pieces can an equilateral triangle be divided into?

126. Grains of rice

There once was a king in India whose son was killed in battle. A wise but poor man in his kingdom invented the game of chess to help the king with his grieving. The king enjoyed the game so much that he invited the wise man to his castle and told him that, as a reward, he could have anything in the kingdom that he desired. The wise man thought for a moment and then said that since his village sometimes did not have enough food, he would like a good amount of rice.

When the king asked him how much rice he would like, the wise man stated his answer as a puzzle. He said that a single grain of rice should be placed on the first square of the chessboard (which has a total of 64 squares). Then two grains of rice should be placed on the second square, and then double that amount (4 grains) on the third square, and double that amount (8 grains) on the fourth square, and so on up to the last square – square No. 64. That is how much rice he would like – if the king didn't feel that the request was too great. He warned the king that all the rice wouldn't fit nicely on the chessboard, but that didn't really matter – he just wanted that amount of rice. The king thought to himself that the wise man was actually quite a fool since he could have had anything in the kingdom, and he was only requesting a few bags of rice.

a) How many grains of rice are there on the whole chessboard (assuming that it would somehow fit)?

b) How many 12 kg sacks of rice would this be, and if all these sacks were laid in a line end-to-end, how far would they stretch? (Each sack is 50 cm long and contains around 400,000 grains of rice.)

c) What is the volume of the rice? (Hint: There are about 400 grains of rice in a 15 mℓ tablespoon.)

The second part of the story, below, should only be told after the students have worked on the above questions.

The king ordered his servants to go into the royal kitchen and carry out the wishes of the wise man. However, once they reached the 23rd square, they came to the king and told him that they had run out of rice in the kitchen. The king was surprised, but told them to take as much rice as needed from the royal granary. The servants worked for two whole days bringing rice from the granary. They then approached the king and told him that they had emptied the entire royal granary and had only reached the 39th square. The king was quite shocked. He asked how much more rice would be needed, and the royal astronomer said that he had calculated that it was far more rice than had ever been produced in the entire world.

The king laughed as he realised that he had been tricked. He then approached the wise man and asked him what he would really like to have, and the wise man said that his greatest wish was to marry the king's daughter. The king thought that the wise man was worthy, so the marriage took place the next day.

Upper School Puzzles

Geometric Puzzles

127. Slicing a hexagon

How can a hexagon be cut into 4 pieces such that those pieces form two equilateral triangles?

128. The snail's journey

A snail crawled up the outside of a cylindrical water tower, which is 7 metres tall and has a circumference of 2.4 metres. However, in order to make his journey easier, he crawled up at a slight (but constant) incline such that by the time he made it to the top, he had circled the water tower exactly 7 times. How far did he actually travel?

129. Making a square

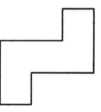

The figure shown on the right has only right angles, and each edge has a length of either 1 cm or 2 cm. How can you make two straight cuts such that the three resulting pieces can be arranged to form one square?

130. A shaded region

Given that the two squares, shown here, have sides of length 8 and 5, find the area and perimeter of the shaded region.

131. Connected circles

The squares, shown here, have sides of length 14 cm and 34 cm. What is the length of the line that joins the centres of the inscribed circles?

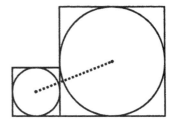

132. Nested polyhedra

If you have a cube with a tetrahedron and an octahedron inside it, what is the ratio of their volumes?

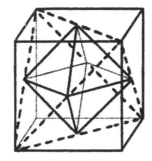

133. Paths on a globe

From which places on the earth can you travel 1 km south, 1 km east, and then 1 km north, thereby ending up back at your origin? How many total such places are there? (*Hint:* It is more than one.)

134. Four points

Given four random non-coplanar points in space, how many planes are equidistant from all four points?

135. Three vertical lines

With the diagram shown here, the lines marked as 10, 15, and x are all parallel. Find x.

(It is interesting to note that if the base of the figure were lengthened or shortened, the value of would not change.)

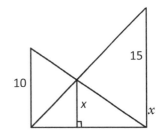

136. Connecting twelve dots

Without lifting your pencil off the page, and ending up back at the place where you started, draw five lines that pass through all 12 of the points in the 4-by-3 grid shown here.

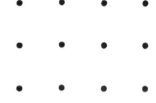

137. Leonardo da Vinci's lunes

Given that there are three semi-circles shown in this drawing, what is the sum of the areas of the two lunes, L and M? Express your answer in terms of the other variables.

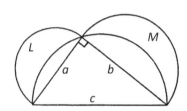

138. Pythagorean quadruples

Pythagorean triples are the three sides of a right triangle, where all three sides (a, b, c) work out as whole numbers. The well-known formula that relates these three lengths is $c^2 = a^2 + b^2$. We can instead relate this to a rectangle, where a and b are the lengths of the sides of the rectangle, and c is the length of its diagonal. Now, taking this idea into three dimensions, we have a right rectangular prism (that is, a box), where a, b and c are the length, width and height of the prism, and d is the body diagonal of the prism. We have a Pythagorean quadruple when all four lengths turn out to be whole numbers.

a) Find the length of the diagonal of a prism that has dimensions (a, b, c) equal to 8, 9, and 12. (This should yield a Pythagorean quadruple.)

b) Give a formula that relates a, b, c and d.

c) Find as many Pythagorean quadruples as you can.

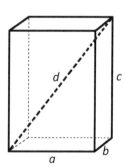

139. Squares and circles

With the drawing shown here, the side of the outer square has a length equal to 1, and the two arcs are each a quarter of a circle. Find the length of the side of the smaller square, and the radii of the two circles.

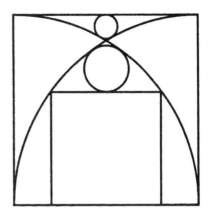

140. Three shadows

A straight rod is embedded in a solid rectangular block made of transparent plastic. The sun is directly overhead. From a random corner, label the three faces which meet at that corner as *A, B, C*. When face *A* is placed on level ground the length of the shadow of the rod is 5 cm. When face *B* is placed on the ground the shadow's length is 6 cm, and when the face *C* is placed on the ground, the shadow's length is 7 cm. How long is the rod?

141. Four intersecting circles

This drawing shows a square with four quarter-circle arcs. Find the area of the shaded region, given that the square has an edge of length 1.

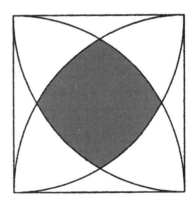

Algebraic Puzzles

142. Four numbers in a square

If four non-zero digits are placed in the box, four two-digit numbers are produced (if you read both vertically and horizontally). The sum of these four two-digit numbers is 65. What are the digits in the box?

143. Age puzzles

a) Sue is 11 times as old as Paul. When Paul will be twice as old as he is now, Sue will be how many times older than Paul?

b) The following is an ancient riddle about the Greek mathematician Diophantus.

Diophantus passed one sixth of his life in childhood, one twelfth in youth, and one seventh more as a bachelor. Five years after his marriage, his son was born. How old was Diophantus when he died if his son died four years earlier and lived to be half as old as his father did?

144. Brothers and sisters

George and Emily are siblings. George has twice as many brothers as sisters, and Emily has three times as many brothers as sisters. How many children are in the family?

145. A herd of cows

One-fifth of Cathy's herd of cows is in the barn. One-third is in the pasture. A number of cows equal to twice the difference of the first two groups is drinking in the stream. The remaining 18 cows are wandering in the forest. How many cows are there in the whole herd?

Fun With Maths Puzzles, Games and More

146. Two-digit numbers

a) What two-digit number is twice the sum of its digits?

b) Two two-digit numbers are such that their digits are the reverse of one another and the ratio of the two (two-digit) numbers is 7:4. Find the numbers.

c) There are 2 two-digit numbers. The larger number is greater than 50, but the smaller number is not. The smaller number is a prime number, but the larger number is not. The sum of the two numbers is 10 less than twice the larger number. The sum of the second digits of both numbers is less than 11. What are the two numbers?

147. House painting

A man hires three men to paint his house. The first painter boasts that he can paint the house himself in just 6 hours, the second says he can do it in 4 hours, and the third can do it in 3 hours. How long would it take all three painters to do the job if they all worked together?

Note: The following three 'maths magic tricks' are great attention-grabbers for Classes 4 to 7. Now, in the Upper School, we can use algebra to show why these tricks work.

148. Guessing one number

The teacher says to a group of students: 'Choose any number, write it down, and circle it. Add 7. Multiply by 3. Subtract the original number. Tell me your final answer.' After hearing each student's final answer, the teacher can then determine what the student's original number must have been. Use algebra to determine how the teacher can do this.

149. Guessing two numbers

The teacher says to a group of students: 'Choose any two numbers (smaller is easier!). Write down the smaller one first, and then the larger one. The third number in your list should be what you get when you add together your first two numbers. You get your fourth number by adding together the second and third numbers. The fifth number is equal to third and fourth numbers added together. Now, carefully add up all five numbers. Subtract from this sum twice your second number. Tell me what number you now have.'

The teacher then says: 'Now take the answer that you just gave me and subtract from it, ten times your first number. Tell me what number you now have.'

After hearing each student's two results, the teacher can then determine what the student's original two numbers must have been. Use algebra to determine how the teacher can do this.

150. Guessing three numbers

The teacher says to a group of students: 'Think of any three single-digit numbers (except zero), in any order, and write them down. Once you have chosen your three numbers, multiply the first number by two, add five, and then multiply by five. Now add the second number, subtract four, multiply by ten, add three, and then add the third number. Now tell me your final result.'

After hearing each student's final result, the teacher can then determine what the student's original three numbers must have been. Use algebra to determine how the teacher can do this.

151. Average speed

Loren leaves home for work at the same time every day. If she drives to work at an average speed of 75 km/h, then she arrives two minutes early. If her average speed is 65 km/h, then she arrives two minutes late. How far does Loren drive to work?

152. More average speed

Ben had to drive from his home to his office, and then back again along the same route. He got stuck in traffic on the way from his home to the office, so his rate of speed was only 10 mph. Determine the rate that he has to drive from the office back to his home in order for the average speed for the whole trip (back and forth) to be exactly

a) 20 mph

c) 18 mph

b) 15 mph

d) 21 mph

153. The leopard and the dog

A dog is ⅜ of the way across a bridge when he spots a leopard running at him from behind. If the dog runs toward the leopard, attempting to escape that way, he will be caught at the near end of the bridge. If he runs away from the leopard, he will be caught at the far end of the bridge. If the dog always runs 15 km/h, how fast must the leopard be running?

154. Crossing ripples

A man drives a boat at a constant rate in a straight line across a calm pond. A fish jumps directly ahead of him, sending out an ever-growing ripple on the surface of the pond. From the instant that the ripple started, he goes (along the same straight line) for 12 m before he crosses the ripple the first time, and another 12 m before he crosses the same ripple again. How far was he from the fish when it jumped?

155. Sums of multiples

Find the sum of all the numbers from 1 to 1000 that are multiples of either 5 or 3.

156. Clock hands

When are the minute and hour hand of a clock *exactly* together between four and five o'clock?

157. The itinerant monk

On Saturday, starting at 7 am, Bob the monk hiked 6 km to a temple at the top of a mountain. After spending the rest of the day and the next night at the temple, he woke the next morning (Sunday), and, at 7 am, started his hike back down the mountain, along the same trail as the previous day. The ratio of his walking speed uphill to his speed downhill is 2:5. Both speeds were constant. How far from the temple was he when he was at the exact same place at the same time on the two different days?

158. A shepherd's flock

Upon death, a shepherd designated that his herd of sheep must be divided in the following way: The first son has one sheep and then one-seventh of what is left; the second son has two sheep and then one-seventh of what is left; the third son has three sheep and then one-seventh of what is left, and so on, until the last son. It turned out that each son ended up with an equal number of sheep. How many sheep were in the original herd? How many sons were there?

159. The horrific age puzzle

Note: I first gave this puzzle to my ninth grade class as an April Fool's joke. It was only later that I discovered, much to my surprise, that it actually can be solved.

Eleven years from now, Alex will be 4 times as old as Craig was, when Beth was 3 times as old as Alex was, two years ago. Beth is 8 years older than half as old as Craig will be, when he is 3 years younger than Alex will be, when Beth will be twice as old as Alex will be, 7 years from now. When Alex was two years old, Beth was 4 years older than Alex will be, when Craig will be one year younger than 3 times as old as Beth was, 7 years before the time when Craig was half as old as Alex will be, when Beth will be 14 years older than she was, when Craig was one-sixth as old as a year more than Alex was, when Beth will be 4 times as old as she was, when Craig was born.

How old is each person now?

Fun With Maths Puzzles, Games and More

160. Dogs on a triangle

Note: This is really a Class 11 or 12 problem.

Three dogs start out such that they are located at the vertices of an equilateral triangle, having 90 m long edges. The dogs start running after one another, such that each dog runs directly toward the dog on his left, thereby following a curved path. If each dog runs at a constant rate, how far do the dogs run before meeting each other at the centre of the original triangle?

Logic Puzzles

161. Three men
There are three men – Don, Ron and Lon – two of whom are married, two have brown eyes, and two are bald. The one with hair has blue eyes. Don's wife is Ron's sister. The bachelor and Lon have the same colour eyes. Which man has hair?

162. Saints and crooks
In a certain village everyone is either a saint (who always tells the truth), or a crook (who always lies). Two men, Bob and Bill, who are both from this village, approach you. Bob says, 'At least one of us is a crook.' What are Bob and Bill?

163. Labelling boxes
There are three boxes. One box contains two apples; one box contains two mangos; and one box contains a mango and an apple. Labels were made indicating the contents of each box, but someone put the labels on incorrectly. Consequently, each box has the wrong label on it. Your job is to figure out which label belongs with each box. You get to select one box, and then someone will show you a random piece of fruit from that box. This is your only clue. Come up with a strategy which guarantees that after seeing the one piece of fruit (your only clue), you can state with certainty which label belongs on each box.

164. Dominoes on a chessboard

You have 31 dominoes, and a standard (8-by-8) chessboard, except that one square from the top-left corner has been removed, and so has the bottom-right square. Each domino is a rectangle that perfectly covers two squares of the chessboard. Is it possible to cover the 62 squares of this chessboard with the 31 dominoes? If yes, then show how this can be done. If no, then give an explanation or proof for why it can't be done.

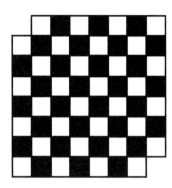

165. Two sisters

Of the three girls Ann, Betty and Christy, two are sisters. The taller of Ann and Christy is the younger sister. The shorter of Ann and Betty is the older sister. The younger of Betty and Christy is the shorter sister. Which of the two girls are sisters?

166. Five hats

Five boys (A, B, C, D, E), each with a hat on that is either yellow or red, stand in a circle looking at one another. Each boy cannot see the colour of his own hat, but can see the colour of all the other hats.

   Boy A says, 'I see three yellow hats and one red hat.'
   Boy B says: 'I see four red hats.'
   Boy C says: 'I see three red hats and one yellow hat.'
   Boy E says: 'I see four yellow hats.'

   Determine the colour of each boy's hat given that every boy with a red hat always tells the truth, and every boy with a yellow hat only tells lies.

167. The wizard and the old man

A wizard demanded that an old man give him either his daughter or his son in payment for a debt. The old man could not decide what to do, so the wizard said, 'We shall decide it in this way. You must say one sentence. If what you say is true, you must give me your daughter. If what you say is false, you must give me your son.' The old man agreed to this plan, thought for a moment, and then said, 'I will give you my son.' What then happened?

168. The two-door riddle

Ben is trying to escape from an evil castle. He comes to a room that has two doors next to one another. If he opens one door he will die; the other door leads to his freedom, but he doesn't know which door is which. There are two guards: one always tells the truth and the other always lies, and Ben doesn't know which one is the liar and which one is honest. Ben may ask only one question to one of the guards. What question should he ask in order to guarantee his freedom?

169. A and X

The figure here must be filled in so that each row of four circles contains two *As* and two *Xs*. Which circle *must* be filled with an A?

170. Stolen chocolate

Somebody stole Bob's chocolate bar. Jerry, Mary and Larry were suspected. Jerry said, 'I didn't do it!' Mary said, 'Larry didn't do it!' And Larry said, 'Yes, I did!' At least two of them lied. Who stole the chocolate bar?

171. Three suitors

A princess had three handsome, charming, and highly intelligent suitors whom she could not choose between, so she held the following contest. The three suitors were brought into a private room. They were shown five small pieces of silk, all identical, except that two were yellow and three were green. They were then each blindfolded (with a piece of cloth) and one piece of silk was randomly chosen for each suitor, and fastened to the back of his shirt. The suitor that could first correctly guess the colour of his own piece of silk would be declared the winner.

The first suitor had his blindfold removed, and he saw the colours of the other two suitors' silks. He then approached the judge and whispered his guess of the colour of his own silk so that the others couldn't hear him. It was then announced that the first suitor was wrong, so he was dismissed from the room.

The second suitor had his blindfold removed, and he saw the colour of the last suitor's silk, approached the judge, and whispered his guess of the colour of his own silk. It was then announced that he too was wrong, so he was dismissed from the room.

Before having his blindfold removed, the third, and final suitor announced that he was now certain of the colour of his silk, stated what colour it was, and, being correct, thereby won the princess's hand in marriage.

What was the colour of the third suitor's silk, and how was he able to be certain of it?

Brain Teasers

172. A very large hotel

On the first day of August, only one room in a hotel was full. On the second day, two rooms were full. On the third day, four rooms were full. And on the fourth day, eight rooms were full. So it continued, doubling the number of full rooms, until, on the last day of August, the hotel was exactly full.

a) How many rooms are there in the hotel?

b) On what day did the hotel become half full?

173. Buckets

You have two buckets. One measures exactly ten litres, and the other measures exactly three litres. You can use as much water as you need, but you may only use these two buckets. How can you measure out exactly one litre of water?

174. Four people crossing a bridge

Abe, Bob, Kate and Mary come to a bridge in the middle of the night. At most, two people can cross at the same time, but they must cross at the rate of the slower person. Individually, Abe takes two minutes to cross, Bob takes ten minutes to cross, Kate takes one minute, and Mary takes five minutes. There is only one flashlight, and it must be used for all crossings. What is the least amount of time necessary for all four people to make it across the bridge?

(*Hint:* It can be done in less than 19 minutes.)

175. Two hourglasses
There are two hourglasses. One runs for 7 minutes, and the other runs for 4 minutes. How is it possible to time a 9-minute interval?

176. Fish bowl
A fish bowl contains 200 fish. 99% are goldfish and the rest are guppies. How many goldfish must be removed in order to be left with 98% goldfish?

177. Stick puzzles
Note: There are many more wonderful stick puzzles in the sections for Classes 6, 7 and 8. It may be best to start with those somewhat easier stick puzzles before doing the ones found below.

With each puzzle, every stick must be part of a square or triangle. No two sticks may be placed on top of each other or side by side.

a) Move three sticks so that you end up with exactly two squares.

b) Shown here is a stick figure of a fish, which is swimming to the left. Move three sticks so that you end up with a fish that is swimming to the right.

c) Move three sticks so that you end up with exactly three squares.

d) Given a hexagon with six triangles, move two sticks so that you end up with exactly five equilateral triangles.

e) Given the same hexagon with six triangles as above, move four sticks so that you end up with exactly four equilateral triangles.

f) Given the same hexagon with six triangles as above, move four sticks so that you end up with exactly three equilateral triangles.

178. Ages of teenagers
There is a group of teenagers. The product of their ages is 737,100. Find the number of teenagers in the group and the age of each one.

179. Magic cubes
a) Number the vertices of a cube 1 to 8 so that the vertices of any face have the same sum.

b) Number the vertices of a cube 0 to 7 so that every connecting edge always has a prime sum. (Remember that 1 is not a prime number.)

c) Number the edges of a cube 1 to 12 so that the faces and parallel edges (which come in groups of four) always have a magic sum of 26.

180. A long rope
Imagine that there is a rope going around the equator of the earth. The rope is exactly 100 metres longer than the equator (which is about 40,000 km long), and the rope is somehow suspended everywhere at an equal height above the surface. Could a horse jump over the rope?

181. Equal products

With the configuration on the right, each letter stands for a different (single) digit. Assign values to the letters so that $A \times B \times C$ and $B \times D \times E$ and $F \times E \times G$ are all equal.

A		F
B	D	E
C		G

182. A square and a triangle

With each figure below, fill in the circles so that each row of three circles has the same sum. (Each circle must be filled in with a different number.)

a)

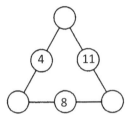

b)

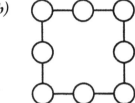

183. Pentagram and hexagram

With the figures below, fill in the circles so that each row of four circles has the same sum.

a)

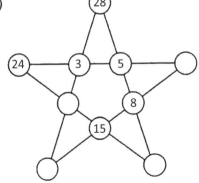

b)

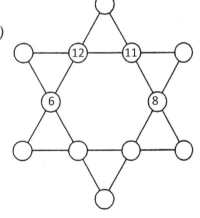

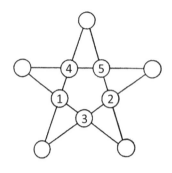

184. Magic star
Fill in the pentagram shown here so that the sum of each diagonal is 20.

185. Connect-the-dot triangles
How many possible *non-congruent* triangles can be formed by connecting three of the dots on this four-by-four grid in order to make a triangle?

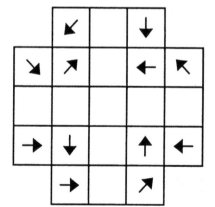

186. The chess king
A chess king can move one space in any direction (eight different directions, including diagonals). Show how a king can make a tour of all 21 squares (hitting each square only once) on this board, with no direction being repeated in any row or column, and ending up back where you started. Part of the board has already been filled in for you.

Fun With Maths Puzzles, Games and More

187. The three lights

There is a room (without windows) which has three lamps sitting on a table. You are outside the room where there are three light switches, each switch controlling one of the lamps. Come up with a plan that allows you to determine which switch controls which light, provided that you can only go into (or look into) the room once.

188. Crossing a desert

You are on the edge of a desert that is 800 miles wide. There is an unlimited supply of fuel at the start. Your truck can carry enough fuel (in its tank and in jerrycans) to travel exactly 500 miles. At any point along the route, you may remove as much fuel as you like from your truck, put it in jerrycans, and leave it in the desert.

a) In order to cross the desert, what is the minimum number of times needed to return to the start to pick up more fuel?

b) What is the largest desert that can be crossed?

189. Blood test

Jeff took a blood test and tested positive for a disease that is known to occur, on average, in 1 person out of 100,000. The blood test is known to be 98% accurate; specifically, 2% of the time there will be a false positive (that is, someone without the disease will test positive for the disease). What is the probability that Jeff actually has the disease? What does this say about the test?

190. Tiling a courtyard

A rectangular courtyard can be covered exactly by 1440 square tiles. If each tile were 2 cm longer and wider, the courtyard could instead be covered exactly with 1210 tiles. Find the dimensions of the courtyard. (The tiles may not be broken into pieces.)

191. All triangles are isosceles?

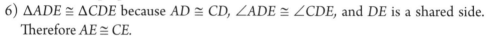

The following proof shows that all triangles are isosceles.
Find the error.
1) Let $\triangle DABC$ be any triangle.
2) Draw the perpendicular bisector of AC.
3) Draw the angle bisector of $\angle B$.
4) Let point E be the point of intersection of the perpendicular bisector of AC and the angle bisector of $\angle B$.
5) Draw EG such that it is perpendicular to AB. Draw EF such that it is perpendicular to BC.
6) $\triangle ADE \cong \triangle CDE$ because $AD \cong CD$, $\angle ADE \cong \angle CDE$, and DE is a shared side. Therefore $AE \cong CE$.
7) $\triangle GBE \cong \triangle FBE$ because $\angle GBE \cong \angle FBE$, $\angle BGE \cong \angle BFE$, and BE is a shared side. Therefore $EG \cong EF$ and $BG \cong BF$.
8) $\triangle GAE \cong \triangle FCE$ because $EG \cong EF$, $AE \cong CE$, and $\angle AGE$ and $\angle CFE$ are both right angles. Therefore $AG \cong CF$.
9) $AG + BG = CF + BF$, and $AB = BC$
10) $\triangle ABC$ is isosceles!

192. A square from nowhere

With the shapes above, all of the vertical and horizontal lengths are either 1, 2, 3, 5, or 8. Every angle that looks like a right angle is a right angle. If we rearrange the four pieces, we get the configuration on the below, which has the exact same overall height (5), and length (13) as the original (top) shape.. How is it that the small black square hole appears?

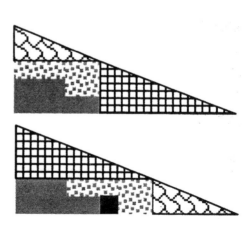

193. The prisoners' dilemma

One afternoon, the prison warden tells 20 prisoners that they will be blindfolded and marched out to the courtyard the following morning. Once there, they will be lined up (with everyone facing forward, towards the person directly in front of him) and a red or blue hat will randomly be placed on each head. The blindfolds will be removed, and beginning at the back of the line, each prisoner, in turn, will be allowed to say only the word 'red' or 'blue'. If he correctly states the colour of his own hat, he will be set free. If he says the wrong colour, he will not be freed.

Each prisoner can see all the hats in front of him, can hear what the prisoners before him have said ('red' or 'blue'), as well as the announcement that follows stating whether that prisoner is freed or not. The prisoners have the whole previous night to come up with a plan that will free the most prisoners. What is the best plan?

(There is no certain number of red or blue hats. Once the prisoners are placed in line, they may not communicate with one another in any way, other than by saying 'red' or 'blue' when his turn comes. We shall also assume that all of the prisoners are highly intelligent, and therefore can follow any coherent plan.)

194. The three daughters

A clever man said to a clever girl, 'I have three daughters. The product of their ages is 72, and the sum of their ages is the same as your age.'

The girl sits down and thinks about it. After a while she said, 'I still need more information.'

'OK,' said the man. 'My oldest daughter is shorter than you.' Then the girl quickly and correctly gives the ages of the man's three daughters.

What is the age of each daughter?

195. Weighing coins

a) You have 12 coins and a balance scale. All of the coins are gold and weigh exactly the same, except a fake one, which is slightly lighter. Devise a plan to discover which coin is the fake, in at most three weighings.

b) (A more difficult variation) You have 12 coins and a balance scale. One coin is a fake, but you don't know whether it's heavier or lighter. Devise a plan to discover the fake coin, in at most three weighings.

196. A hidden card

Your partner is sent out of the room. A dealer hands you five cards from a standard 52-card deck. You look at the cards and hand them back to the dealer, one by one, in whatever order you choose. The dealer takes the first card that you hand her and places it face up, in a spot labelled 1. The next three cards that you hand her, she places, similarly, in spots labelled 2, 3, 4. The last card that you hand her goes face down, in a spot labelled 'hidden'. Your partner enters the room, looks at the four face-up cards, and the spots in which they lie, and from that information, correctly states what the hidden card is (both the suit and the value).

The question is: What is the foolproof scheme that you and your partner settled on ahead of time? (While you control the order of the cards, you have no control over their orientations, so you can't use that to transmit information to your partner.)

197. Money and a circle

Several people, each one with a certain whole number of pounds, sat in a circle. Initially, the first person had one pound more than the second, who had one pound more than the third, and so on. The first person gave one pound to the second, who gave two pounds to the third, and so on, each giving one pound more than he or she received, perhaps going several times around the circle. Everything stopped once one person was not able to pass along one more pound than he received. At that point, there was a person who had four times as much as his neighbour. How many people were there? How much money did the poorest person have to begin with?

198. Careful handshaking

Three very important heads of state are set to meet and shake hands for photos with the president. At the last minute, just before the ceremony, the secret service is tipped off that one person is an impostor with a deadly substance on his hand. The ceremony must go on; there is no time to discover the impostor. They find that they have only two single discreet rubber gloves to use for the three handshakes. The president will not wear one for the photo. How can they ensure that no one will come in direct or indirect contact with the substance when they don't know who the impostor is?

Problem-Solving Exercises

Note: The problems in this section are mostly designed for Classes 11 or 12.

199. Rolling a one

The game simply goes like this: All of the students stand. The teacher rolls two dice. As long as no 1s are rolled, everyone receives a score equal to the sum of the two dice. Some students may choose to sit down (keeping their current score) if they fear that the next roll will show a 1. The two dice are rolled again, and if a 1 is rolled on either die, then everyone standing ends up with a score of zero. If a 1 isn't rolled, then everyone standing has their score increased by the sum of the two dice, and then they need to decide if this is now the right time to sit, or not. The game continues until a 1 is rolled or until nobody remains standing. The game should be played a few times to give the students a sense of the game.

The question we ultimately want to answer is: what is the best strategy in order to maximise your average score per game?

200. Monty's choice

On an American game show (*Let's Make a Deal,* similar to *Trick or Treat* in the UK) the contestant was always given the choice of three doors (A, B or C). A new car was hidden behind one of the doors, and a joke prize (for instance, a goat) was behind each of the other two doors. The contestant would state which door he chose, hoping that behind the door would be a new car. But Monty Hall, the game show host, who knew what was behind each door, would *always* then open one of the other doors – a door that didn't have the car behind it. Then he would offer the contestant the chance to switch his choice to the other remaining door.

The question before us is: Does switching (as opposed to sticking to the original choice) increase, decrease, or leave unchanged, the probability of winning a car?

201. Two ants

And here is a problem in feet and inches (remember, there's 12 inches in a foot).

a) Two ants (one male, one female) are at diametrically opposite corners inside a box that measures 2 × 2 × 5 ft. What would be the length of the shortest path, walking from one ant to the other?

b) The male ant is on the front square wall of the box, equally far from each of the rectangular side walls and 2 inches from the ceiling. The female is diametrically opposite the male – that is, on the back wall, 2 inches up from the floor, and equally far from the side walls. How long is the shortest path that goes from one ant to the other?

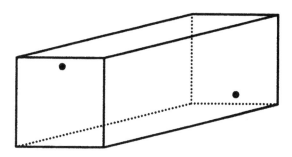

c) Where would the two ants be situated such that they are as far apart as possible? (The distance between any two points is the shortest path that can be walked by an ant, from one point to the other point.)

d) If the male ant is at the left top front corner of the box, where would the female ant need to be situated in order to be as far away as possible from the male ant? (*Hint:* It's close to, but not exactly on, the diametrically opposite corner.)

202. Lines and points

Draw 4 lines on a page, as shown here, such that they all intersect on the page, but no three lines are coincident.

Fairly easily, we can see that 6 points of intersection are formed, and that, from these 6 points, 3 new lines can be drawn (by connecting any two of the 6 points).

Starting instead with 10 lines on the page, how many points of intersection are there, and how many new lines can then be drawn using any two of these points of intersection?

203. Cut plane

Ten planes divide space into how many regions? (No two planes may be parallel; any three planes must intersect at exactly one point; no four planes may meet at the same point, etc.)

204. The dartboard

A dartboard is divided into twelve equal-sized, pie-wedged regions, one of which is the 'target'. Assume that each thrown dart has an equal chance of landing in any of the twelve regions. The objective is to hit the target region. Darts will continue to be thrown until one dart hits this target.

a) What is the probability that the number of throws needed to hit the target is exactly 3 throws?

b) What is the probability that the number of throws needed to hit the target is 3 throws or less?

c) What is the expected (average) number of throws needed to hit the target?

d) The Dartboard Principle. What law can be stated about the above problem?

205. Baseball cards

Note: This problem may involve writing a simple computer program.
In the United States Dan is collecting baseball cards. Every day at the store he buys one packet, which contains five random cards. There exists a total of 200 different cards. What is the expected (that is, average) amount of time for Dan to collect all 200 cards? Assume no trading! (*Hint:* It may be helpful to use the above Dartboard Principle.)

206. Hitting ten

You toss a coin repeatedly. Heads is worth 1 and tails is worth 2. You add up the score as you go along. What is the probability that you'll have a score of 10 along the way (that is, not skip over 10)?

207. Four sons

Note: This problem may involve writing a simple computer program.
An old man had four sons who asked for some money before they set forth into the world. The man decided to distribute the money in the following manner. He took his entire life savings of gold coins and gave the first son 4 coins, and then gave him one quarter of what remained. Then he went to the second son and gave him 4 coins, and one quarter of what remained. He then he did the same with the third and the fourth son. What is the fewest number of coins that the old man could have started with?

(Assume that every time he took one quarter of what remained there was no remainder?)

208. Secret Santa

Note: This problem may involve writing a simple computer program.
In a class of 25 students, each student is to draw the name of a fellow student out of a hat in order to determine his or her secret Santa. What is the probability that no student will draw his own name?

209. Prime factorisation

Note: All of the problems here can be solved through the use of prime factorisation.
a) 109,350 is not a square number, but if it is multiplied by a certain number, then the result is a square number. Find the smallest number that makes this possible.

b) Factorials certainly get large very quickly. If you were to multiply out 4273!, how many zeroes would it end in?

c) 14 has four factors (including 1 and itself), 60 has twelve factors, and 48 has ten factors. But how can we determine the number of factors of any given very large number? For example, it turns out that the number 1,103,350,248,000 has 3360 factors. (How did I figure that out?) How many factors does 9,489,150,000 have?

d) Give at least one number that has exactly 6 factors.

e) Give at least one number that has exactly 10 factors.

f) Give at least one number that has exactly 7 factors.

g) Give at least one number that has exactly 9 factors.

h) Give at least one number that has exactly 13 factors.

i) Give at least one number that has exactly 15 factors.

Fun With Maths Puzzles, Games and More

210. Angles in a star polygon

It is well known that the sum of the (interior) angles of a polygon can be calculated by the formula $s = 180 \times (n-2)$, where s is the sum of the angles, and n is the number of sides of the polygon. But this is something different.

a) Find the sum of the star point angles of this heptagon (7 points), which is created by connecting every third point on the circle.

b) Find the sum of the star point angles of the heptagon below, which is created by connecting every second point on the circle.

c) Would your answers to the above two questions be different if the heptagon were not regular (that is, the points were not evenly spaced on the circle)? Explain why.

d) Find the sum of the star point angles of a heptadecagon (17 points), which is created by connecting every eighth point on the circle.

e) Find the sum of the star point angles of a heptadecagon, which is created by connecting every third point on the circle.

f) Determine a formula (or method) by which you can calculate the sum of the angles of any star polygon, where n is the number of points of the star, and every x number of points along the circle is connected in order to create the star polygon.

Games

211. I've got your number!

Class 5–9
Number of players: 10+
Maths required: multiplication facts
Time to learn: 10 minutes
Time to play: 15 minutes
Target situation: whole class activity

This is a great game for practicing factoring and multiplication. Though it is competitive, students can continue to play even after they are eliminated. The game has a clever mechanism whereby students have to do repeated calculations to win, but they are never put on the spot in front of their classmates. It can work for a class of almost any size.

Rules

Have the students make a circle with their chairs and give the following instructions.
    'Stand next to your chairs.
    'Pick a number from 1 to 9; keep it to yourself.
    'You will hear me call different numbers. If your number is a factor of the number I call, step on top of your chair. Once you are there, if your number is a factor of the next number I call, step down. Again, go up and down *only* if your number is a factor of the number I call. For example, if you picked 2, and I call 13, you do not move, 14, you go up, 16, you go down, etc.

'After I have called 5 numbers, you can guess which number any of your classmates has picked, if you are wrong, you have to sit down, and continue guessing from your chair. If you are right, that classmate has to sit down and is out of the game.

'We will continue to play until there are only 4 players left.'

Example

The students pick as follows: Ann (2), Bob (4), Cathy (6), Douglas (8), Eddie (9), Frank (3).

Teacher calls '24.' Ann, Bob, Cathy, Douglas and Frank step up.

Teacher calls '12.' Ann, Bob, Cathy, and Frank step down. Douglas remains on his chair.

Teacher calls '10.' Ann steps up.

Teacher calls '16.' Ann and Douglas step down. Bob steps up.

Teacher calls '18.' Ann, Cathy, Eddie and Frank step up.

Since 5 numbers have been called, the teacher calls for guesses. Frank guesses Alice is 2, and Alice sits down. Bob incorrectly guesses that Eddie is 3, and Bob sits down.

The game continues.

Notes

To make the game more challenging, the allowable factors can be expanded to include 10-19.

Even after they are eliminated, students are allowed to make guesses about the numbers of players still in the game. If they are correct, that player is eliminated.

Occasionally, I will have students who do not want to play because they are not confident in their ability to identify allowable factors. I usually suggest that they pick the number 2 or 5 until they feel more confident.

212. Century whist

Class 5–9
Number of players: 4
Maths required: addition
Time to learn: 15 minutes
Time to play: 20 minutes
Target situation: small group

This is a card game for four players using a special deck of cards.* It is played in partnerships of two like bridge or whist. The rules are simple enough so that the players will not need much oversight from a teacher. Once explained, one should be able to engage a full class playing it in groups of four. The calculations that result are significant. Students must consider many possible addition problems on any given turn.

The deck

The deck consists of 50 cards numbered 0 to 9. You can purchase special maths decks, but it is much easier to create your own special deck by using two decks of standard cards, as described below.

Take one complete suit from deck 2 and add it to deck 1. Deck 1 should now have 65 cards. It is best if the card backs are the same, but not absolutely necessary. Discard the rest of deck 2. You only need deck 1 from here on.

Remove all the Kings, Jacks and Tens from deck 1. It should now contain 50 cards.

Aces count as 1 and Queens count as a zero. Suits are irrelevant. Only the number on the card matters.

---

* This game, called 'Hekaton', is from Sid Sackson's *A Gamut of Games*. The game was created for a special deck of cards called the Yankee Notion Cards in the mid-nineteenth century. These cards were manufactured so pious Americans would not have to use a standard deck of cards which were thought to be immoral Devil's Picture Books.

Fun With Maths Puzzles, Games and More

Rules

The four players sit in a circle. A player's partner sits opposite her in the circle.

Twelve cards are dealt to each player. The remaining two cards are placed on the table as the start of the first trick. The player to the left of the dealer starts.

Each player lays down a single card in turn until a card is laid such that the collection of cards on the table can be arranged as a multiple of 100 (e.g., 200, 3800, etc.). There are two possible ways to arrange the cards.

A *single number* (for instance, the cards 4, 8, 0 and 0 can be arranged as the number 8400 or 4800). Or the *sum of two or more numbers* (for instance, the cards 9, 1, 4 and 5 can be arranged as the sum of $91 + 4 + 5$).

Whenever this occurs, the 'trick' is won, and the team scores the value of the number. The person to the left of the trick's winner starts the next trick. Play continues until all the cards are played. If a trick remains incomplete after the last person plays her card, that trick is not scored. Cards are shuffled and re-dealt. Play continues until a team scores 10,000 points.

There is a special rule about zero cards (Queens) and creating sums. Whenever a zero already has been played, you can assume a zero in any other number that is part of the sum (see example C below).

Examples

A) Two cards have been played in the trick – 6 and 0. The player plays a 0 card and wins the trick as she has created the number 600. Her team scores 600 points.

B) Three cards have played in the trick – 3, 6 and 8. The player plays a 2 and wins the trick by creating either of the following sums:

$32 + 68 = 100$ or $62 + 38 = 100$.

The player's team scores 100 points.

C) Two cards have been played in the trick – 6 and 0, but the player doesn't have a zero. She can win the trick by playing a 4 and imputing the second zero:

$60 + 4(0) = 100$.

The player's team scores 100 points.

D) Five cards have been played in the trick – 4, 5, 5, 6, and 7. The player wins the trick by playing an 8:

657 + 45 + 8 = 700.

The player's team scores 700 points.

Notes

Once students get the hang of combinations that win tricks, the game becomes highly strategic. The goal is usually to put down a card that the next player will be unlikely to use to win the trick but will be very useful to your partner.

You can make 4 Century Whist decks with 5 standard decks of cards. Since 4 children play with one deck, a class of 32 children would need 8 Century Whist decks or 10 standard decks.

213. Skedoodle

Class 5–9
Number of players: 2–3
Maths required: the four processes, plus squares and roots
Time to learn: 10 minutes
Time to play: 5–15 minutes
Target situation: small group

This pencil and paper game uses only basic arithmetic.* But playing it well, and planning several moves out to see the ramifications, requires the same will in thinking that is needed for mental maths. Best of all, it's fun and slightly addictive.

*   Skedoodle was invented by a Benedictine monk, Father Daniel, who lived in Wisconsin, USA in the middle of the twentieth century. It was popularized by Sid Sackson when he included it in his book, *A Gamut of Games*. Tos use chess as an example, it is fairly easy to picture what a chess board will look like after you move a single piece, but it is rather difficult to do this beyond 3 or 4 moves, even if the moves are all pretty simple.

Fun With Maths Puzzles, Games and More

Rules

Before the game, the players agree on two things: the 'magic digit', and the range of allowable numbers. The magic digit can be any whole number between 3 and 9. The range of allowable numbers can be anything the players want up to 99. A good range for starters is 1–30. You can make the game more challenging (and longer) by expanding the range.

The object of the game is to score the most points. You score a single point by creating a 'scoring number', and you score two points if you make the final move of the game (that is, the player following you cannot create a number in the allowable range).

Scoring: you create a scoring number if your number
— has the magic digit in it,
— or if the magic number can be reached by adding, subtracting, dividing or multiplying the digits of your scoring number.

Moving. The first player chooses any number in the allowable range, provided it is not a scoring number. The next player creates a new number from this number by
— manipulating the digits by +, −, × or ÷,
— doubling the number,
— halving the number,
— squaring the number,
— or taking the number's square root.

The new number created must be a whole number that has not been used yet in the game. The number 1 is a special case; it can be used to move to any other number. Play continues until a player cannot make a move because there are no allowable numbers left from the current number.

Example game

Magic Digit: 6 *Range:* 1–30 *Players:* 3

Player 1: 3

Player 2: Moves to 6 by doubling. (Scores 1 point because number contains magic digit.)

Player 3: Moves to 12 by doubling.

Player 1: Moves to 24 by doubling. (Scores 1 point because digit addition on 24 gives 6. Note that the player cannot move to 6 because that number has already been used.)

Player 2: Moves to 8 by digit multiplication.

Player 3: Moves to 4 by halving.

Player 1: Moves to 16 by squaring. (Scores 1 point because number contains magic digit.)

Player 2: Moves to 7 by addition.

Player 3: Moves to 14 by doubling (only move).

Player 1: Moves to 5 by digit addition.

Player 2: Moves to 25 by squaring.

Player 3: Moves to 10 by digit multiplication.

Player 1: Moves to 1 by digit addition.

Player 2: Moves to 26 by special 1 rule. (Scores 1 point because number contains magic digit.)

Player 3: Moves to 13 by halving (only move).

Player 1: Moves to 2 by digit subtraction. Only move. Scores two points since now Player 2 has no allowable moves. Digit addition, subtraction, multiplication, and division are not possible. Halving gives 1 (already played). Doubling and squaring give 4 (already played). Square root of 2 is not a whole number.

Score: Player 1 = 4 pts; Player 2 = 2 pts; Player 3 = 0 pts

Notes

Players can play to a certain number of points over several games.

This game invites rule tinkering. This should be encouraged and new variations should be shared with classmates. A common variation is to allow a move by adding or subtracting 4 to the current number.

With a younger class, it is helpful to write down all the allowable numbers at the beginning of the game and then cross them off as they are used. In addition, you can circle all the scoring numbers at the beginning of play.

214. Rithmomachy

Class 5–9 (Class 6 is ideal)
Number of players: 2
Maths required: the four processes
Time to learn: 30 minutes
Time to play: 30 minutes
Target situation: small group

This is probably the most famous game you have never heard of. The name comes from the two Greek words rithmos 'number' and mache 'battle'. From the eleventh to the sixteenth centuries, it was the most popular board game of the intellectual class in Western Europe. Its decline, in the late fifteenth century, seems to coincide with the rise of the Chess of the Mad Queen, which today is simply known as chess.

I will present a simplified set of rules that I think would be appropriate for a Class Six.* Even so, the amount of time needed to teach this game and to have the students

---

* The rules ramble a bit like a medieval treatise. For example, there are eight different ways to win a game. Five are grouped under the heading of 'Common Victories' and the three are the 'Proper Victories'. More complete rules can be found in *The Oxford History of Board Games* by David Parlett. They are also available online at *www.gamecabinet.com/rules/Rithmomachia.html*.

create the boards and pieces would make it impossible to do just as a maths class activity. However, given that it was the most popular game of medieval Europe, it might make a good tie-in to the Class Six medieval main lesson block.

Rules

Board and pieces. Rithmomachy is played on an 8 × 16 checkered board. The easiest way to create one is to put two chessboards end to end. Pieces are in three different shapes – round, triangular, and square. Each piece has a number on it.

The pieces are arranged as shown.

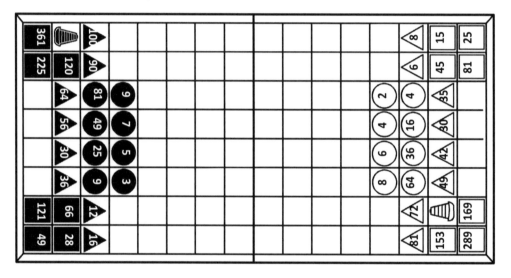

Both players have one 'pyramid' piece, which is a stack of round, triangular, and square pieces. For the white player, the pyramid is a square 36, square 25, triangular 16, triangular 9, round 4, and round 1. The white pyramid has a total value of 91. The black pyramid is a square 64, square 49, triangular 36, triangular 25, and a round 16 with a total value of 190.

Moving. Players move one piece per turn. Pieces move in a straight line in any direction but may not jump over other pieces (like a knight in chess). Round pieces must move one square; triangular pieces must move two squares; and square pieces must move three squares. At the end of a move, a piece exerts a 'zone of control' equivalent to any square it could legally move to on the next move. There can be no intervening pieces in between for another piece to be in a zone of control. This is important for capturing.

Pyramids can move according to any of the movement rules of the pieces in the stack. Pyramids can separate by moving only some of the pieces in the stack. Once a pyramid separates, it cannot be rejoined.

Capturing. When a piece is captured, it is removed from play. There are four methods of capture.

— *Blockade:* the enemy piece has no legal moves because it is blocked in every direction by your pieces or the edge of the board.

— *Equality:* at the end of the move, an enemy piece with the same value is in your zone of control. For instance, white moves his 49 triangle so that only one empty square separates it from black's 49 square. Because white could move his triangle to the space now occupied by black's 49 square on his next move, black's 49 square is captured by equality.

— *Piece arithmetic:* At the end of your move, the value of two or more pieces can be added, subtracted, divided or multiplied to equal the value of an enemy piece that is in the zone of control of all the attacking pieces.

— *Distance multiplication/division:* An enemy piece has a value equivalent to your piece multiplied/divided by the distance between you. There can be no intervening pieces in between and the distance must be a straight line. Note that you always count squares starting with the one your piece is on. As such, if you are adjacent to another piece, you are a distance of 2 from it. For example, at the end of your turn, your 25 triangle is 9 squares away from the enemy 225 square (that is, there are 7 empty spaces between the pieces). The enemy 225 square is captured by distance multiplication.

A *pyramid's value* is the sum of all the pieces therein, whether it is being used to capture or is being attacked. The zone of control of a pyramid is any valid move range for a piece in the stack.

End of game. The game is over when one player captures five or more enemy pieces whose sum exceeds 150.

Notes

This game has a long history and many variations. There are much more involved and complicated sets of rules if the students take an interest.

The creation of wooden Rithmomachy boards and pieces would make a good woodworking project for older students. It would be particularly satisfying because the students would be making something that is unavailable in stores today.

215. Line of four

Class 5–9
Number of players: 2
Maths required: multiplication
Time to learn: 5 minutes
Time to play: 10 minutes
Target situation: small group

This is a fun little game that is perfect for working on multiplication facts. If students have mastered these, then they can enjoy the strategic choices of the game even more.

Equipment

This game requires 38 checkers: 18 black, 18 white, and 2 red. (Coins can be used instead of checkers.)

Game Board

1	2	3	4	5	6
7	8	9	10	12	14
15	16	18	20	21	24
25	27	28	30	32	35
36	40	42	45	48	49
54	56	63	64	72	81

① ② ③ ④ ⑤ ⑥ ⑦ ⑧ ⑨

Rules

The first player places the two red checkers on any digit(s) in the octagons above. She then multiplies the two digits and covers the product on the grid above with her checker (black or white). For instance, if the red checkers are on the octagons 5 and 6, then a black or white checker is placed on the square 30 in the grid. Note that the red checkers are allowed to be placed on the same octagon.

The second player moves one of the red checkers to a new octagon number and then covers the appropriate *new* square in the grid (the product of the two red checkers) with his checker.

Play alternates in this manner until one player has four checkers in a row vertically, horizontally or diagonally.

Notes

The game board can be scrambled into a different order.

The game works well as a whole class activity with one half playing the other. A game board can be constructed using a large piece of poster board.

There is a substantial advantage to the player who moves first. Here are two alternate rules that mitigate this imbalance:

— The first player places only the first red checker. The second player then places the second red checker and places the first (white or black) checker on the grid.

— The first player places both of the red checkers, and places the first (white or black) checker on the grid. The second player has the option to either accept the first player's move and continue play as normal, or to take the first player's move as her own.

There is a challenging variation of this game called 'Line of Six'. In order to play it, you must use playing pieces that are white on one side and black on the other (like in the game Othello). The object of the game is to have a line of six checkers in a row, but there is an additional rule for moving. If you place a checker at the end of a continuous row of your opponent's checkers so that it is bordered at each end by your checkers, you turn over your opponent's checkers to be your colour. (This is a familiar procedure to those who have played the game Othello or Reversi.)

The strategy for Line of Four usually revolves around controlling centre squares; this is reversed in Line of Six where it becomes important to control the edge squares where checkers are less easily flipped.

216. Bizz-buzz
Class 5–9
Number of players: 5+
Maths required: multiplication
Time to learn: 5 minutes
Time to play: 10 minutes
Target situation: whole class activity

This is a very simple game that requires no setup or pieces. This is a battle of nerves and results in a good deal of laughter; it's a wonderful out-breathing activity.

Rules

At the beginning of the game, you decide on two forbidden numbers. The students all stand in a circle. A student starts by saying 'One,' the person to his left says 'Two,' and it continues clockwise. The catch is that a student may not say any number that is a multiple of any of the two forbidden numbers – you must say the appropriate substitute word ('Bizz' or 'Buzz') instead. If the number is a multiple of more than one forbidden number, you must say each of the substitute words. If a student fails to substitute the correct B-word or hesitates, he is out of the game. The game proceeds until only four players remain. When a player is eliminated, the counting starts over again, from 1, with the player to his right.

Example

Bizz = 11, Buzz = 7.

'One,' 'Two,' 'Three,' 'Four,' 'Five,' 'Six,' 'Buzz,' 'Eight,' 'Nine,' 'Ten,' 'Bizz,' 'Twelve,' 'Thirteen,' 'Buzz,' 'Fifteen,' 'Sixteen,' 'Seventeen,' 'Eighteen,' 'Nineteen,' 'Twenty,' 'Buzz,' 'Twenty-two' ...

Play stops here as 22 is a multiple of 11 (the answer should have been 'Bizz'), and that player is eliminated. The counting starts again from 1.

Notes

It is important that there is a rhythm to the counting so that the game moves along.

When introducing this game, it is best to start with only one forbidden digit and call the game 'Bizz'. Once the students get the hang of it, you can add 'Buzz'.

For an even greater challenge, you can add a third multiple and the word 'Bing'.

217. Nim

Class 5–9
Number of players: 2+
Maths required: addition/subtraction, pattern recognition
Time to learn: 5 minutes
Time to play: 2 minutes
Target situation: whole class activity or 2 players

This is the simplest of games and one of the most elegant.* It can be played by two people with toothpicks or with pencil and paper. A chalkboard and an eraser also make a suitable playing arena. The game has an unbeatable winning strategy. Older students quickly realise this, and the point in playing becomes figuring out the winning strategy.

Rules

Game set-up. Sixteen toothpicks are laid out in the following pattern.

```
            I
         I  I  I
      I  I  I  I  I
   I  I  I  I  I  I  I
```

Players alternate turns. With each turn, a player takes as many toothpicks as he wants from just one row. He must take at least one toothpick. Whoever takes the last toothpick loses.

---

* There are many variations of Nim. They all centre around the idea of taking pieces from one or more stacks. This variation is known as Marienbad because it is featured in the artistic film *Last Year at Marienbad (L'Année dernière à Marienbad)*.

Example

After starting with the game set-up, Player No. 1 takes 2 toothpicks from the third row.

```
                    I
                  I I I
                    I I I
            I I I I I I I
```

Player No. 2 then takes 6 toothpicks from the fourth row.

```
                    I
                  I I I
                    I I I
                          I
```

Player No. 1 takes 3 toothpicks from the second row.

```
                    I


                  I I I
                          I
```

Player No. 2 takes 2 from the third row.

```
                    I


                       I
                          I
```

Player No. 1 takes 1 from the third row, and Player No. 2 takes 1 from the first row. Player No. 1 must pick up the remaining toothpick. Player No. 2 is the winner.

Notes

The best way to get a feel for the strategy is to play. A willing opponent is available online. (There are many websites where you can play Nim: a good version is available at *www.archimedes-lab.org/game_nim/play_nim_game.html.*)

It is not necessary to go into the strategy with the students, particularly not for the younger classes.

This game is good to teach right before holiday breaks. It is easy to learn and requires few props. It might get taken up during a long car trip or in the corner at a holiday party.

If you get confident with the winning strategy (see below), it is great to introduce this game by playing against the whole class. It is likely that you will win consistently, no matter who goes first. This will plant the seed that there is a trick.

Strategy

There are two *winning endgame configurations*. If you leave two toothpicks in two rows (and no toothpicks anywhere else) at the end of your turn, you should win. Also, if you leave only one toothpick in three (or five) separate rows (and none in the remaining rows) at the end of your turn, you will win. Additionally, if you leave only one toothpick in two (or four) separate rows (and none in the remaining rows), you will lose. Try these two endings a few times.

There are several ways to explain the winning strategy for Nim.* One explanation connects nicely with Class Eight binary numbers. It is highly unlikely that a student would ever come up with this particular explanation even if she did find the winning strategy. However, it can be followed by the students, and it works!

To find the winning move, count the number of toothpicks in each row and convert the number to a binary number. When your turn is over, you want there to be an even number of 1's in each of the binary place values.

---

* For a detailed explanation that does not use binary numbers, see *The Mathematics of Games* by John Beasley, pp. 99–101.

Fun With Maths Puzzles, Games and More

The exception to this winning strategy is when each row has either one toothpick left or no toothpicks left (see *winning endgame configurations,* previous page).

If both players follow the winning strategy, whoever goes first loses!

In order to understand the above strategy, it should be helpful to see the above game replayed.

Again, we see the game set up at the beginning.

	Decimal	Binary	4	2	1
I	1	001	0	0	1
I I I	3	011	0	1	1
I I I I I	5	101	1	0	1
I I I I I I I	7	111	1	1	1

At the start of the game, there are two 1s in the 4s place, two 1s in 2s place and four 1s in the 1s place. Assuming that both players know the winning strategy, we can say that since there are an even number of 1s in each of the place values (of the binary numbers), the player who goes first should lose.

To start the game, Player No. 1 chooses to take 2 toothpicks from the third row.

I	001
I I I	011
I I I	011
I I I I I I I	111

Player No. 1 has finished his turn with an odd number of 1s in the 4s place and the 2s place. He is in a losing position.

Player No. 2 takes 6 toothpicks from the fourth row.

I	001
I I I	011
I I I	011
I	001

Player No. 2 has finished her turn with four 1s in the 1s place and two 1s in the 2s place. She is in a winning position.

Player No. 1 takes 3 toothpicks from the second row.

```
I                      001
                       000
I I I                  011
        I              001
```

Player No. 1 has finished his turn with an odd number of 1s in the 2s and 1s places. He is again in a losing position.

Player No. 2 takes 2 from the third row.

```
    I


      I
        I
```

This is one of the two 'endgame configurations' that we mentioned above. Therefore, Player No. 2 should win.

218. Three to fifteen

Class 5–9
Number of players: 2+
Maths required: addition
Time to learn: 5 minutes
Time to play: 2 minutes
Target situation: whole class activity or 2 players

This is a simple game to learn, but there seems to be no easy path to victory. Your students will be scratching their heads wondering how you keep beating them.

Rules

The object of the game is to be the first player to choose three numbers that add up to fifteen from the numbers 1 to 9. Players alternate in choosing numbers. Each number can only be selected once. It is possible that the game ends in a tie.

Example

Player A chooses 2; Player B chooses 7.
Player A chooses 5; Player B chooses 8 (to stop player A from getting 2 + 5 + 8).
Player A chooses 4; Player B chooses 9 (to stop player A from getting 2 + 4 + 9).
Player A chooses 6; and wins $(5 + 4 + 6 = 15)$.

Notes

The game can be played by writing the numbers on pieces of paper, or by using playing cards (ace to nine) to represent the nine numbers.

Like the previous game Nim, the fun in this game is figuring out the strategy. Let the students play for a couple of days and see if they can guess the 'secret'.

Strategy

Surprisingly, this is a game of Noughts and Crosses in disguise. Consider the following Noughts and Crosses board/magic square.

You can add up to 15 with three numbers in any one of eight ways, but it is usually best to use '5' since there are four different sums that use it.

4	9	2
3	5	7
8	1	6

219. Glib chap

Class 5–9
Number of players: 2+
Maths required: logic only
Time to learn: 5 minutes
Time to play: 2 minutes
Target situation: whole class activity or two players

This is a variation on the previous *Three to fifteen* game that uses words instead of numbers.

Rules

The object of the game is to be the first player to choose three words that share the same letter from a list of nine words. The nine words are *glib, chap, aloe, dyes, pier, quad, spot, sulk, and void*. Players alternate in choosing words. Each word can only be selected once. It is possible that the game ends in a tie.

Notes

In the classroom, you could list the nine words on the chalkboard and then have the players write their choices on a piece of paper. You could also write the nine words on index cards, which could then be handed out to students. A final option is to list the words on a game board (as below) and cover them with different coloured stones or coins.

glib	chap	aloe	dyes	pier	quad	spot	sulk	void

Example

Player *A* chooses 'pier'; player *B* chooses 'glib'.

Player *A* chooses 'aloe'; player *B* chooses 'dyes' (to stop player *A* from getting 'dyes' and three 'e').

Player *A* chooses 'spot'; player *B* chooses 'chap' (to stop player *A* from getting 'chap' and three 'p').

Player *A* chooses 'void' and wins (with three 'o').

Strategy

Again, this is Noughts and Crosses in disguise. The diagram shows that 'aloe' is in the middle because it can be used in four different winning combinations.

spot	chap	pier
sulk	aloe	glib
dyes	quad	void

220. Trader

Class 7+
Number of players: 15+
Maths required: basic algebra
Time to learn: 10 minutes
Time to play: 30–45 minutes
Target situation: small group

There are many games that work on the basic arithmetic skills like addition and multiplication, but there are few that can map onto algebra. This game gives students the chance to solve algebra equations as part of game play.* It is an excellent game for involving all of the students – the more the merrier – but it will require at least 30 minutes to play a full game.

* Trader is an adaptation of the adult party game Haggle from Sid Sackson's book *A Gamut of Games*.

Rules

The objective of the game is to turn in the most valuable set of chips at the end of the game. There are 5 different colours of chips; each colour chip has a different value. The catch is that the players do not know the chip values at the start of the game. At the start, each student receives the same set of 20 coloured chips and two secrets about the game. Each secret is either an equation about the value of the chips or a rule for scoring the game. Players trade chips and/or secrets for a specified time and then turn in their chips. The player who turns in the most valuable set of chips is declared the winner.

Equipment

For each student playing, you will need:
6 index cards – 5 distinct coloured cards and 1 white one
1 envelope

Preparation

Cut each of the 5 coloured cards into quarters and place them in the envelope. Each envelope should contain 20 cards – 4 of each colour.

As the teacher, you should make up one secret for each player in the game, before class. A secret can be either an equation about the value of the coloured cards or a special scoring rule (see Examples opposite).

Write each secret two times on a white index card and cut the card in half. You should now have twice as many secret cards (each the size of half an index card) as you have players in the game.

Place two secret cards in each player's envelope making sure that the player does not receive two copies of the same secret.

Fold the back over the envelope so the contents do not fall out, but do not seal it.

Play

Give each student one envelope and announce that trading has now begun. Players can trade chips, secret cards or just information. Because of the secret scoring rules, a player cannot be sure she has the best combination of chips unless she gets access to all of the secrets.

Example

Here is an example of the contents of the information cards for a game of 20 students:

All of the point values are prime numbers.

Three reds plus one point are equal to 2 blues.

The least common multiple of the blue value and the white value is 187.

The value of orange is the only even number.

Pick any number. Multiply it by the value of yellow. Take the digits of this product and add them together. The sum will be divisible by the value of yellow.

Blue's value has digits that are the same.

The sum of all the colour values is 40.

The product of the value of orange, yellow and white equals the product of the values of blue and red plus 25.

The value of red is 7.

The sum of the values of orange, yellow and red is one more than the value of blue.

You can score no more than 3 white cards.

A maximum of 15 cards can count towards you score. If you enter more than 15, cards will be removed randomly from your envelope until it contains 15 cards.

If anyone turns in 5 or more blue cards, the value of blue becomes 1 point for everybody.

If you turn in the maximum amount of allowable cards divided equally among the colours, you score double.

Three blues plus a point equals the value of two whites.

Blue – Red = Red – Yellow.

Whoever turns in the most yellow cards gets a bonus of 50 points. If there is a tie, the tied players count their blue cards, and the player with most blue cards gets the bonus. If that is tied, no bonus is given.

Whoever turns in the second most orange cards, gets a bonus of the number of orange cards turned in multiplied by itself. In case of a tie, the tied players see who has the second most red cards. If that is tied, the bonus is divided among the players with the most orange cards.

The sum of yellow and orange multiplied by the sum of yellow and white is 100.

White has the highest value.

The values of the cards for this game would be:

White	17
Blue	11
Red	7
Yellow	3
Orange	2

Notes

This is a spirited game. It can get a little noisy. It is particularly fun to watch the trades change as new information becomes more common.

At least one of the rules should limit the number of chips a player can turn in. You want to encourage students to have to find the most valuable combination of a small set of chips. Simple hoarding of as many chips as possible should never win.

It takes a while to score the game, so usually the winner will have to be announced the following day. Do not announce the value of the chips until then. This encourages the children to discuss information and try to figure out the chip values in the interim.

This might be an interesting game to try in teams.

Fun With Maths Puzzles, Games and More

221. Black box

Class 9–10 (10 is ideal)
Number of players: 2+
Maths required: deductive reasoning
Time to learn: 15 minutes
Time to play: 10 minutes
Target situation: whole class activity or 2 players

Black Box is a game that requires the players to follow a line of deductive reasoning in order to find the location of four hidden balls.* It is described below as a two-person pen and pencil game, but it could be a teacher-led classroom activity.

Rules

One player is the Hider; the other is the Finder. The Hider draws an 8 × 8 grid and places four balls within the 64 cells. He keeps his sheet hidden from the Finder. The rows and columns are numbered from 1 to 32 (see overleaf). Only one ball can fit in a cell.

The Finder draws an identical 8 × 8 grid. The Finder will try to deduce the position of the balls by shooting 'rays' into the box and observing where the rays exit the box as reported by the Hider.

The Finder can stop shooting rays and guess the position of the 4 balls at any time. The Finder can shoot a maximum of 20 rays.

If a ray hits a ball, the ball absorbs the ray. If a ball passes within one space of a ball, the ray is deflected 90° away from the ball.

Special rule: if a ball is located on the outermost row or column of the box and a ray is shot immediately adjacent to it, the ray is reflected to the shooting square.

---

* Originally this was a board game released by Milton Bradley in the mid-1970s. It was adapted to a pencil and paper game in Andrea Angiolino's book *Super Sharp Pencil & Paper Games.*

Examples

A ray that enters at 10 would directly hit the ball and would not exit the box.

A ray that enters at 15 would exit at 19.

A ray that enters at 30 would cause a double deflection and would exit at 30.

A ray that enters at 1 would pass through and exit at 24 (not pictured).

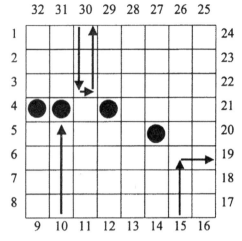

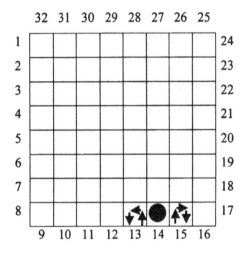

A ray shot at 13 will exit at 13, and a ray shot at 15 will exit at 15. (This is due to the 'special rule' as stated previously.)

Scoring

The Finder scores 5 points for each ball position she guesses correctly.

The Finder scores 5 points for each mistake the Hider makes in reporting where a ray exits.

The Finder loses one point for each ray she shoots into the box that is absorbed or exits the same point it entered.

The Finder loses 2 points for each ray she shoots into the box that exits at a different point than it entered.

Fun With Maths Puzzles, Games and More

After a round, the players reverse roles and play again.

Highest score wins.

Notes

This game is quite good for demonstrating how your assumptions can get you into trouble when not proven through deductive reasoning.

The game can get pretty frustrating when the Hider makes a mistake in reporting where the rays comes out. This is the reason for the 5 point per error rule. The game becomes very difficult for the Finder if the Hider intentionally tries to give incorrect reports.

222. Decatur hold 'em

Class 9–12

Number of players: 6–14

Maths required: probability

Time to learn: 30 minutes

Time to play: 20+ minutes

Target situation: whole class activity

As any poker professional will tell you, poker is first and foremost a game of mathematical probability. Unfortunately, much of maths is useless to the novice because of the incomplete nature of his information. He doesn't know what cards his opponent holds, so he can't be sure of his mathematical chances. It takes a lot of experience in poker before a player can start to make reasonable judgments about his opponents' cards and thus get to the maths of the matter.

Decatur Hold 'Em shortcuts this process by giving the players enough information to calculate probability, but leaves enough of the game intact, so it is still fun. It could be played by Class 9 students in the Permutations, Combinations and Probability main lesson block, or by Class 11 students for a good exercise in analysis.

This is a special adaptation of poker, in general, and the game Texas Hold 'Em, in particular. (If you've never played poker, you should read the rules for poker first before attempting this game.) It is best for 8–12 players, so for a large class, you might have students play in teams of 2. It requires a standard deck of 52 playing cards and some poker chips (about 15 per player should do).

Rules and play

Every player antes 1 chip. Each player is dealt two cards face up, so that all the other players can see them. Two community cards are dealt face up to the centre of the table. The player to the dealer's left has the first option to check, bet or fold. Thereafter, each player has the option to call, raise, or fold (just like regular poker).

<table>
<tr><td>

Check means you chose not to bet or fold. You can only check if another player has not already bet.

Bet means you are increasing the pot and all other players have to do so in turn to stay in the hand.

Fold means you do not want to meet a bet made and are leaving the hand.

Call means that you meet the bet made by the previous bettor.

Raise means that you meet the current bet and increase it; all players must meet your new bet to stay in the hand.

</td><td>

Poker Hands from best to worst

Straight Flush: same suit and in sequence

Four of a Kind: 4 cards of the same rank

Full House: 3 of the same rank plus a pair

Flush: all cards are the same suit

Straight: all cards are in sequence

Three of a Kind: 3 cards of the same rank,

Two Pair: 2 sets of one pair

One Pair: 2 cards of the same rank

High Card: highest ranked card (the highest ranked card is an ace)

</td></tr>
</table>

The maximum bet and/or raise is 1 chip. After the bets are made, the dealer deals one more community card to the centre of the table. Whoever has the best 5-card hand by combining their own 2 cards and the 3 community cards, wins the pot.

You can play as many hands as you like. If a student runs out of chips, she should watch the rest of the hands from the sidelines.

Example

A ten player hand is dealt as follows.

Player 1: 10♠, 7♠ (Dealer)
Player 2: 10♣, 8♣
Player 3: Q♠, 10♥
Player 4: A♦, 6♥
Player 5: Q♣, 4♥
Player 6: Q♦, 3♣
Player 7: 9♥, 3♥
Player 8: K♥, 5♥
Player 9: J♦, 8♦
Player 10: 7♣, 6♠
Community Cards: K♦, 3♦
Pot contains: 10 chips

Here is how the players should play:

Players 2 to 7 should check since Player 8 has the best hand (a pair of Kings).

Player 8 should bet 1 (the maximum bet). Pot = 11.

Player 9 should call. (He will win if any diamond comes up. There are 7 diamonds left in the deck of 30 cards. The probability of winning the pot of 12 is 23.3%. The probability of losing one chip is 76.7%. Expectation = $12 \times \frac{7}{30} + (-1) \times \frac{23}{30} \approx 2.03$ chips. Pot = 12)

Player 10 folds (There is no card that he could come up so that he would win).

Players 1–3 fold for the same reason.

Player 4 calls. (She will win if an ace comes up. There are 3 outstanding, so her expectation is 0.4 chips.) Pot = 13

Players 5 folds.

Player 6 folds. (He can only win if a 3 comes up. Expectation = −0.5 chips)

Player 7 calls (4 winners – a 3 or one of three 9s. Expectation = 1 chip) Pot = 15.

Final community card: 2♣.

Player 8 wins with a pair of kings.

Notes

Setting the maximum bet to 1 is the main factor in making most of the bets callable. Once players get used to this, you can raise the maximum bet to 5 and see who realises this.

The game could be expanded to use 5 community cards with 2 betting rounds – one after the first 3 community cards are dealt and a final round after the fourth community card.

Fun With Maths Puzzles, Games and More

Maths Magic Tricks

Note: These maths magic tricks are great attention-grabbers and are especially effective in Classes 4–7 to help develop a sense of wonder for numbers. Then, years later, in a Upper School algebra course, the problems can be revisited as an interesting algebra exercise to show why a given maths magic trick works.

223. Reversing digits

The teacher says, 'Choose any three-digit number. Create a second number by reversing the digits of the first number. Find the difference of these two numbers by subtracting the smaller number from the larger. This difference must be greater than 100. (If it isn't greater than 100, then start over from the beginning and choose a new initial number.) Reverse the digits of this difference and add this number to the difference itself.'

Amazingly, the final number will always be 1089!

Example

Choose 826. The second number is therefore 628. The difference is 198. Reversing the digits of the difference gives us 891. And, lastly, 891 + 198 equals 1089.

224. Number circle

The teacher says, 'Choose any two-digit number. Double it. Add 7. Multiply it by 5. Add 13. Multiply by 10. Subtract 480. Divide by 100.'

The final number will always be the same as the number you started with.

As an added challenge, have students invent similar problems on their own.

225. Upside down addition

The teacher says, 'Write down these numbers in a column and add them: 986, 808, 969, 989, 696, 616. When you are finished, write down the same numbers again in a column, and turn the paper upside down. You should notice that these numbers can all be read. Some of them are the same as before, and some are different. Now add these numbers together.'

In both cases, the column of numbers should add to 5064.

226. Guessing one number

The teacher says, 'Choose any number, write it down, and circle it. Add 7. Multiply by 3. Subtract the original number. Tell me your final answer.'

The teacher can then take the student's final answer, subtract 21, and then divide by 2. The result is the student's original number.

227. Guessing two numbers

The teacher says to a group of students, 'Choose any two numbers (smaller is easier). Write down the smaller one first, and then the larger one. The third number in your list should be what you get when you add together your first two numbers. You get your fourth number by adding together the second and third numbers. The fifth number is equal to the third and fourth numbers added together. Now, carefully add up all five numbers. Subtract from this sum twice your second number. Tell me what number you now have.'

The teacher then says, 'Now take the answer that you just gave me and subtract from it, ten times your first number. Tell me what number you now have.'

The teacher can now determine what each student's original two numbers are just by knowing the student's two results. The teacher simply adds the student's two results and divides by ten in order to get the second number in the student's list. The first number is arrived at by finding the difference of the student's two results and dividing by ten. The teacher can then tell the amazed student what his first two numbers must have been.

228. A list of ten numbers

Start with two numbers between 1 and 9. Add these two numbers together to get a third number. Add the second and third number together to get a fourth number. Add the third and fourth numbers together to get a fifth number. Continue this process until you have ten numbers. Add together all ten numbers. Divide by 11. This final answer will always be equal to the seventh number in your list.

229. Guessing three numbers

The teacher says, 'Think of any three single-digit numbers (except zero), in any order, and write them down. Once you have chosen your three numbers, multiply the first number by two, then add five, and then multiply by five. Now add the second number, subtract four, multiply by ten, add three, and then add the third number. Now tell me your final result and I will guess what your original three numbers were.'

The teacher then subtracts 213 from the end result, which will always produce a three-digit number consisting of the original three numbers.

230. Casting out nines

Normally, we check a multiplication problem to see if it is correct by simply redoing the problem. This is problematic for two reasons: it is time consuming, and we are likely to make the same mistake again. *Casting out nines* allows us to quickly check our answer after doing a multiplication problem. It may be easiest to understand by studying the following example. The key is to realise that the arrows represent summing the digits (for instance, with 7296: $7 + 2 + 9 + 6 = 24$).

If the circled results aren't the same, then there is a mistake in the multiplication. A shortcut for summing the digits is to cast out (from the original two numbers or the answer) all groups of digits that add to nine, or multiples of nine. Thus, with the answer 2743296: the first two digits (27), the next three (432), and then the 9, are all cast out, leaving just the 6 as the result. With practice, this is very quick.

231. The birthday trick

The teacher says the following, 'Think of someone's birthday. Take the number of the birth month (for instance, May is 5) and multiply it by ten. Add eight. Multiply by five. Add 122. Double it. Finally, add the day of the month of the birthday.'

Now the teacher asks one student what his/her ending number is. The teacher takes that number and quietly subtracts 324. The resulting number should be such that the rightmost two digits will be the day of the month, and the digit(s) to the left of that will be the month. The teacher can then announce the birthday that the student was thinking of.

After doing this trick a few times, the students can try to figure out what the teacher's secret is that makes this trick work (subtracting 324 at the end).

232. The chocolate and age trick

Before the teacher states this problem, she must determine x, which is the current calendar year minus 250.

Then the teacher says, 'How many times per week do you like to eat chocolate? Multiply that number by two. Add five. Multiply the number by 50. Add x [*the number she determined earlier*]. If you haven't already had a birthday in this calendar year, then subtract 1. Now subtract the year in which you were born.'

The end result should be a number, where the last two digits are your age, and the digit(s) in front of the age is the number of times per week you like to eat chocolate.

Additional question: Under what circumstances won't this trick work? (It won't work if someone is 100 years old or greater.)

Classroom Activities

233. A right angle with a rope

Class 5 or 6

This is how the Egyptians made a right angle by using a rope. Bring the class into a field and have a rope that is 36 metres long, with a knot tied 15 m from one end and a knot tied 12 m from the other end. (The distance between the two knots should now be 9 m.)

Form a triangle with the rope such that the three corners of the triangle are the two knots and the place where the ends of the rope come together. All three sides of the triangle should be tight and straight. As long as everything has been done properly, the result should be a right triangle. The Egyptians used this method to make right angles. Show that if one knot is moved a few feet, then you no longer get a right angle. This also serves as a prelude to the Pythagorean theorem in Class Seven.

234. Perfect number race

Class 5 or 6

*What are perfect numbers?** In general, a whole number is categorised as abundant, deficient, or perfect based upon the sum of its factors. In order to determine this we first list the number's factors, except for the number itself. Then we sum up the numbers in that list. If this sum is equal to the number itself, then we say the number is perfect. If this sum is less than the number itself, then we say the number is deficient. If the sum is greater than the number itself, then we say the number is abundant.

* Read more on perfect numbers in Jamie York's *A Teacher's Source Book for Mathematics in Classes 6–8*, pp. 220f.

The Race. Show the students that 6 is a perfect number because its factors (1, 2, 3) add to six. Then tell the students that there is only one more perfect number that is less than 100, and have them race to find it. (The answer is 28.)

235. The shadow problem
*Class 7 ***

Choose a narrow, tall object outside to calculate its height (for instance, a tree or a telephone pole). At a moment when there is sun, measure the length of the object's shadow. Take a long pole (or a stick) and measure the height of this pole and the length of its shadow when held vertically next to the tall object.

   Now, draw two triangles – one for the tall object and one for the pole – roughly to scale. With each triangle, one side represents the length of a shadow, one side represents the height, and the third side (which won't be used) represents the line that could be drawn from the top of the object to the end of its shadow. Label these two triangles with the lengths that you measured and label the height of the object (which is what you are trying to calculate) as x. Calculate the height of the object. Round your answer to three significant figures.

236. Determining a value for π
Class 7*

Find a fairly large, nearly perfect circle (for instance, a bike wheel).† Measure, as accurately as possible, the length of the circumference (**C**) and the length of the diameter (**D**). Using long division, calculate the ratio of the diameter to the circumference ($D:C$), and also the ratio of the circumference to the diameter ($C:D$), both in decimal form. Round your answer to three significant figures.

---

*   This exercise also appears in Jamie York's *Student Workbook for Maths in Class 7*, p. 45.
†   This exercise also appears in Jamie York's *Student Workbook for Maths in Class 7*, p. 75.

Fun With Maths Puzzles, Games and More

237. Pythagorean cut-out puzzle

Class 7

With any non-isosceles right triangle, draw a square coming off each of the three sides. (It may be best to have students work in groups, with each group drawing a slightly different right triangle.) Extend two lines from the sides of the largest square so that they cut through the other two squares, in each case dividing the squares into a triangle and a trapezoid.

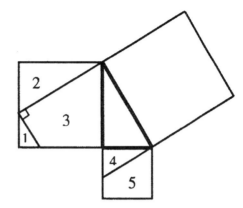

Draw a line perpendicular to the line that divided the second largest square, by starting at the intersection point on the edge of that square. The second largest square has now been cut into three pieces: two triangles and a quadrilateral having two right angles. Cut the 5 pieces out of the two smaller squares. Place these 5 pieces on top of the largest square so that they fit perfectly. This is a great geometric puzzle!

Have the class do this before saying anything about the theorem, and then ask them what the drawing shows.

It shows that the sum of the areas of the two smaller squares equals the area of the largest square, which is the Pythagorean theorem.

238. Creating magic squares

Upper School

One of the puzzles from earlier in this book (No. 58) involved the creation of a 3 × 3 magic square, shown here.

One particularly fascinating magic square is the 4 × 4 magic square (shown overleaf) from Albrecht Dürer's engraving, *Melencolia I.* The sum 34 can be found in the

4	9	2
3	5	7
8	1	6

16	3	2	13
5	10	11	8
9	6	7	12
4	15	14	1

rows, columns, diagonals, each of the quadrants, the centre four squares, the corner squares, the four outer numbers clockwise (or anti-clockwise) from the corners (e.g., 3 + 8 + 14 + 9), the two sets of four symmetrical numbers (e.g., 2 + 8 + 9 + 15), and more! The two numbers in the middle of the bottom row give the date of the engraving: 1514.

Creating a 4 × 4 magic square

Method No. 1

You would think that creating a magic square would be difficult, but it isn't really. Here are instructions that anyone can easily follow.

1. Using your own 4×4 grid, choose any numbers you wish for the shaded boxes, as shown here.
2. Choose any magic sum that you wish. (With Dürer's magic square shown above, the magic sum was 34.)
3. Fill in the rest of the empty boxes of the magic square such that each row, column, and diagonal have a sum equal to your magic sum. Also, the four corners, and the middle four cells should add to the magic sum. (Note that, very likely, some of the numbers will need to be negative.)

Method No. 2

This method is more freeform and interesting, but perhaps a bit more risky. Put a blank 4 × 4 grid on the blackboard. Have the students take turns filling in a single square. With each turn, the student should look at the whole grid and see if there is a particular square that must be filled in with a certain value. If not, the student is free to fill in a random square with a random value. Once again, check to be sure that each row, column, diagonal, the four corners, and the middle four cells all add to the same sum.

Creating a 5 × 5 magic square

Method No. 1

The following procedure can be used to create any $N \times N$ magic square, where N is odd.

1. Choose an arithmetic sequence such that the number of elements in the sequence is equal to the number of boxes in the square. (An arithmetic sequence has equal-sized steps between each number in the sequence.) Possible sequences for a 5 × 5 magic square are:

   1, 2, 3 ... 25

   3, 6, 9 ... 75

   24, 28, 32 ... 120

   −5, −3, −1, 1, 3 ... 43

2. Place the first number of the sequence in the top-middle box of the magic square.

3. Place the next number of the sequence into a box according to the following rules:

   — Move one box up and to the right from where the previous number was entered.

   — If moving up and to the right by one box moves you out of the magic square to the right, the next number should instead be placed one level above the previous entry, but in the left-most column. Similarly, if the move takes you out of the top of the magic square, the next number should be placed one column to the right of the previous entry, but on the bottom row.

   — Any time the next position is already occupied by a number, the next number should instead be placed directly below the previous number.

The diagram here shows the order of the numbers with a 5 × 5 magic square.

17	24	1	8	15
23	5	7	14	16
4	6	13	20	22
10	12	19	21	3
11	18	25	2	9

4. If these directions have been accurately followed, then the median number (which is also the average of the highest and lowest number of the sequence) should end up being placed in the middle of the magic square. Also, the magic sum should be equal to the middle number times the number of columns. (In the square on the previous page, the magic sum is $13 \times 5 = 65$.)
5. Of course, it is good to check your magic square by seeing if each column, row and diagonal actually add to the magic sum.

Method No. 2

This is essentially the same freeform method shown above as method No. 2 for making a 4 × 4 magic square.

Put a blank 5 × 5 grid on the blackboard. Have the students take turns filling in a single square. With each turn, the student should look at the whole grid and see if there is a particular square that must be filled in with a certain value. If not, the student is free to fill in a random square with a random value. Once again, check to be sure that each row, column, and diagonal add to the same sum.

239. Binary hand-raising

Class 8

I often do this at the end of the Class 8 number bases unit. It's a lot of fun, but a basic knowledge of binary is required.

Five students are invited up to the front of the room and stand next to one another. The student furthest to the (audience's) right is the 1s place; the next student is the 2s place; then the 4s place, the 8s place, and finally, the student furthest to the left is the 16s place. If a student has her hand up, then that indicates a '1' in that place.

We begin by asking the students to show us a few numbers. For example, if we ask for 13 (base-ten), then this number is 1101 in binary, so the first, third and fourth students should have their hand up (and the second and fifth students have their hand down).

Fun With Maths Puzzles, Games and More

Now the real fun begins! The teacher counts (in base-ten), at a rate of about one number per second: 'one, two, three, four…'. The students need to raise (and lower) their hands in order to represent those numbers in binary.

For added amusement, three students can represent a six-digit binary number (by using both hands), or two groups of five students can have a race to see which group can get from 0 to 31 the fastest.

240. Deriving the formula for the area of a circle

Class 8*

With a compass, construct 3 circles that have a radius of about 5 cm.* Shade in the inside edge of each circle's circumference with a coloured pencil. Cut the first circle into 4 equal-sized pie pieces, the second one into 8 pieces, and the third one into 16 pieces. In each case, put the pieces side by side alternating top and bottom. The first one should look like this:

Questions to consider:
What happens as the circle is cut into more and more pieces?
What shape results from having the circle cut into infinitely many pie pieces?
What is the area of this final shape?
Therefore, what is the area of the original circle?
What is the formula for the area, *A*, of a circle, given just the radius, *r*?

---

* This exercise also appears in Jamie York's *Student Workbook for Maths in Class 8,* p. 34.

241. Calculating the speed of sound

Class 8

The following activity is designed as a practical activity where the students calculate the speed of sound.

Find a long flat field, or a similar space which allows for a long distance. One student should act as the 'sounder', standing at one end of the field, while the rest of the class stands at the other end of the field.

The distance between the sounder and the rest of the class needs to be measured. One way to measure this distance is with a bicycle – simply walk that distance with the bike and count the number of revolutions of the wheel. (The diameter of the bike wheel also needs to be measured to calculate its circumference.)

The sounder uses a 'banger' which makes a very loud sound that can be seen and heard over the large distance. This banger can be constructed by taking two flat wooden boards (about 25 ×150 mm and 600 mm long) and connecting them at their ends with a hinge. When the signal is given, the sounder smashes the banger together. Several students use stop watches to time the difference between when they see the banger come together and when they hear it. A few trials are necessary in order to get accurate results.

Once back in the classroom, the students should calculate these values:

1) the average of the reasonable times;

2) the distance between the sounder and the timers;

3) the speed that the sound travelled over that distance.

242. Counters

Class 9

The Waldorf science curriculum gives students the opportunity to observe phenomena and draw conclusions about the natural world. These opportunities are rare for the laws of mathematics, but one area where one can experiment and observe mathematical laws is with the laws of probability. Counters is a solitaire game where students can discover the most likely rolls of two dice.

Game board

2	3	4	5	6	7	8	9	10	11	12

How to play

The player is given 11 tokens that she can place on any number or combination of numbers. For example, she could place one token on each number. Alternatively, she could place five tokens on 5, four on 8 and two on 12. The player then rolls two dice. If she rolls a number that has a token on it, she can remove one token. The player continues to roll until she removes all eleven tokens, keeping track of the number of rolls along the way. The object of the game is to remove the tokens in the least number of rolls.

It may be best to have the students work in small groups.

It is best to introduce the game one day and let students play through it a few times. Ask them to develop a strategy for placing the tokens by experimenting and recording their results for homework. The following day ask them what, if any, conclusions they have reached. Have the whole class try some of the suggested strategies and then record the results. It will become clear which strategies might have worked for a student because of a lucky set of rolls and which are effective because they are in alignment with the best probabilities.

243. Calculating a mountain's height

Classes 10–12

In 1852, Radhanath Sikdar discovered that Peak XV was the highest in the world. He then led an effort to calculate the height of this mountain as accurately as possible. Several readings, all taken from the plains of India, were averaged. In 1856 it was announced that the height of this mountain was 29,002 feet. This measurement was within 50 feet.* Sikdar's boss, the General Surveyor of India, Captain Andrew Waugh, named the peak after his predecessor, Sir George Everest.

How could this have been done? Try the following practical exercise.

With a sextant, measure the angle of elevation of a nearby mountain (or a tall building) from a given point on a level field. Then walk forward directly toward the mountain and take a second angle of elevation reading. Be sure to measure the distance between the two points, and make sure that the two points are at a relatively equal elevation.

The solution is found readily using the Law of Sines. This can also be a lesson on error and accuracy, where the students can learn that the further forward they walk to take the second reading, the more accurate the results will be.

244. The equation of a thrown ball

Class 12

The following practical activity nicely brings together many different topics from Upper School maths.

Prerequisites (for the basic questions)
Coordinate geometry: graphing parabolas.
Solving systems of equations: this task involves three equations with three variables.

---

* The height is now reckoned to be 8848 m (29,029 ft).

Prerequisites (for the advanced questions):
Differential calculus: determining the slope of a tangent line.
Vector analysis: determining the horizontal and vertical speed vector components
   of the ball.

Equipment
Net (volleyball or tennis), tennis ball, tape measure, stopwatch, masking tape. A
   video camera is optional.

Procedure
Person No. 1, standing about 10 m from the net, throws the ball (underhand and
   fairly fast) barely over the net. Person No. 1 freezes his hand at the exact place
   where he let go of the ball.
Person No. 2 marks with his hand exactly where the ball was when it passed directly
   over the net. (If a volleyball net is used, person No. 2 ought to be standing on the
   umpire's chair or on a step ladder.)
Person No. 3 marks the point *(C)* where the ball exactly landed on the other side of
   the net.
Person No. 4 uses the stopwatch to measure the flight-time of the ball. (Several
   people with stopwatches would even be better.) It may also be valuable to record
   the flight of the ball on a video recorder.
Using a piece of masking tape, mark (as point *B)* the spot on the court that is directly
   below where person No. 2 shows that the ball passed over the net.
Using a piece of masking tape, mark (as point *A)* the spot on the court that is directly
   below where person No. 1 released the ball.

Measurements needed
The height above the ground that person No. 1 released the ball.
The height above the ground that the ball was when it passed over the net (as
   indicated by person No. 2).

The horizontal distance from the point of release to the net (point *A* to point **B***).
The horizontal distance from the net to the point of impact (point *B* to point **C***).

The questions (roughly in order of difficulty)
What is an equation for the flight of the ball?
What was the position (coordinates) of the ball when it was at a maximum height?
Ignoring the time given by the stopwatch, what was the length of time that the ball
    was in the air? (Compare your answer with the stopwatch time.)
What was the horizontal speed of the ball?
What was the angle at which the ball was thrown?
What was the ball's speed when it was released?

Fun With Maths Puzzles, Games and More

Solutions

Class Four Puzzles

1. Coin puzzles
a) 4 10p and 11 5p coins
b) 24 10p and 6 5p coins
c) 8 20p and 22 5p coins

2. Counting squares
There are 9 small squares, one 3×3 square, and four 2×2 squares, making a total of 14 squares.

3. Form tracing
You have to start either at the bottom-left or bottom-right point of the figure.

4. A basket of fruit
a) The possible answers are one less than multiples of 15 (14, 29, 44, 59, etc.).
b) The possible answers are five less than multiples of 12 (7, 19, 31, 43, etc.).

5. Sums and differences
a) 19 and 5
b) 13 and 11
c) 33 and 20

6. Halfway between
a) 18
b) 37
c) 53
d) 450
e) 755

7. Products, sums and differences
a) i) 9 and 4
   ii) 12 and 3
   iii) 36 and 1
b) i) 12 and 2
   ii) 6 and 4
c) i) 6 and 8
   ii) 12 and 4
   iii) 24 and 2
d) i) 8 and 5
   ii) 20 and 2
e) i) 50 and 2
   ii) 20 and 5

8. Missing-digit arithmetic

a)
```
    458
+   762
   1220
```

b)
```
      47
×     52
      94
+   2350
    2444
```

c)
```
      83
×     54
     332
+   4150
    4482
```

9. Money problems
a) £3.00
b) £215
c) £9.00
d) 15 months
e) 80p
f) 5 rides
g) £50.40
h) Assuming 52 weeks in a year, we get £1456.
i) £11.50
j) 8 weeks
k) £54

10. Measurement problems
a) 21 metres
b) 12 cm
c) 37½ cm
d) 17½ tonnes

11. Measuring a brick
a) 11¼ cm
b) 10¾ cm
c) 21½ cm
d) 4 m 50 cm (or 450 cm)

12. Counting problems
a) 43   *c)* 9
b) 53   *d)* 17

13. Favourite numbers
a) 11   *e)* 14
b) 13   *f)* 8
c) 31   *g)* 37
d) 51

14. Lots of pets
a) 5   *c)* 20
b) 5

Class Five Puzzles

15. Pets' legs
a) Two cats and one bird
b) Six cats and four birds

16. In the middle
There are 19 students in the class.

17. Filling in the boxes
54 × 3 = 162.

18. Triangle flipping
Move the two bottom outside coins up two rows, and move the top coin to just below the bottom row (but keep it in the centre).

19. Counting triangles
Given the original shape and size,

there are five triangles of each of these shapes and sizes:

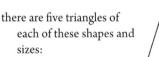

there are ten triangles of each of these shapes and sizes:

Therefore, there are a total of 35 triangles.

20. A cricket ball and a bat
The cricket ball costs £5 (and the bat costs £105).

21. Five odd numbers
27, 29, 31, 33, 35

22. Enough children
There would need to be at least six children – three girls and three boys.

23. Counting racers
a) The possible answers are two less than multiples of 12 (10, 22, 34, 46, etc.).
b) The possible answers are three more than multiples of 20 (23, 43, 63, etc.).

24. My favourite number

It is my favourite number because if we multiply by 2, 3, 4, 5, or 6 the digits are all the same, but just shifted.

a) 285,714   d) 714,285
b) 428,571   e) 857,142
c) 571,428   f) 999,999

25. A clock riddle

a) The answer is 4:45. Fifteen minutes ago it was 30 minutes after 4 o'clock. Now it is 15 minutes before 5 o'clock.

b) The answer is 7:54. A half hour ago it was 24 minutes after 7 o'clock. Now it is 6 minutes before 8 o'clock.

26. A 4 × 4 magic square

7	20	11	12
14	8	23	5
20	6	13	11
9	16	3	22

27. Sums and differences

a) 31 and 19
b) 43 and 7
c) 52 and 37

28. Halfway between

a) $14\frac{1}{2}$
b) 41
c) 389
d) 4,500,000

29. Amicable numbers

The factors of 220 add to 284, and the factors of 284 add to 220. These are called 'amicable numbers', and were known by the Pythagoreans. 284 and 220 are the smallest pair of amicable numbers. The next few pairs of amicable numbers are:1210 and 1184; 2620 and 2924; 5020 and 5564; 6232 and 6368.

30. Coin puzzles

a) 15 20p and 9 5p coins
b) 21 20p and 8 10p coins

31. Products, sums and differences

a) 3, 4, 5

b) i) 10 and 3
   ii) 6 and 5
   iii) 15 and 2
   iv) 6 and 5
   v) 15 and 2

c) i) 10 and 6
   ii) 12 and 5
   iii) 20 and 3
   iv) 20 and 3
   v) 30 and 2

32. Sums of primes

a) 5 + 31; 7 + 29; 13 + 23; 17 + 19
b) 7 + 83; 11 + 79; 17 + 73; 19 + 71; 23 + 67; 29 + 61; 31 + 59; 37 + 53; 43 + 47
c) 2 + 2 + 31; 3 + 3 + 29; 3 + 13 + 19; 5 + 7 + 23; 5 + 11 + 19; 5 + 13 + 17; 7 + 11 + 17; 11 + 11 + 13

33. Age puzzles

a) Jeff is 11 years old.
b) 14 years from now
c) 15 years old
d) Jimmy will be 25 years old.

34. Money problems
a) £6 exactly
b) 13 weeks (he will have saved £505)
c) 26p per roll
d) £1.70

35. Missing-digit arithmetic
a)
```
    348
  + 805
   1153
```
b)
```
       83
    ×  57
      581
  +  4150
     4731
```
c)
```
        78
     ×  45
       390
  +  3120
      3510
```
d)
```
        117
     ×  319
       1053
       1170
  +  35100
      37323
```

36. Fraction problems
a) 186 cm
b) 28⅜ cm

37. Measurement problems
a) 73 times 175 mℓ is 12,775 mℓ. She needs to buy 13 litres.
b) 195 g
c) 5880 kg, 196 boxes
d) 37¼ p at Bob's shop, which is cheaper than Fred's.

38. Lots of pets
a) 9
b) 7
c) 15

39. Unit cost and proportions
a) £6.08
b) £11.48
c) £6.08
d) £5.25
e) 4 hours
f) 25 minutes
g) 4 hours 45 minutes

40. Counting problems
a) £40
b) £17
c) 36 students
d) 44 marbles
e) Suzy had 13 and Ann had 7.
f) 6 cards

Class Six Puzzles

41. Trading cats
The girl has 7 cats and the boy has 5 cats.

42. Trading cards
Keith had 16 and Ben had 8.

43. Comparing money
£112

44. Weighing coins
2.5 kg

45. Cutting a board
5½ minutes (only 11 cuts are necessary).

46. Summing primes
a) 5 + 13 + 23 (there are many other possible solutions).
b) 2 + 3 + 13 + 23 (there are many other possible solutions, but each one must include a 2).

47. The chicken, fox and sack of grain

First he brings the chicken across. Then he returns across the bridge empty-handed and brings the fox across. Once he reaches the other side, he leaves the fox, but takes the chicken back across (to the starting point). He leaves the chicken there, and takes the sack of grain across. He leaves the sack of grain with the fox, and then returns empty-handed across. Lastly, he brings the chicken across the bridge.

48. The hungry cat

14 mice

49. Counting siblings

Four daughters and three sons

50. Giving change

One possible solution is 5 × 1p, 5 × 5p, 3 × 10p, and 2 × 20p.

51. Football games

a) 38 × 20 ÷ 2 = 380. (We divide by two because there are two teams in each game.)
b) 6080 footballs
c) Approximately 2600 kg

52. Stick puzzles *(different solutions shown)*
a)

b)

c)

d) (The horizontal stick has been slid to the right slightly.)

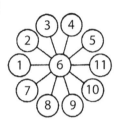

53. Number wheel

There are three possibilities for the middle: 6 is in the middle, with a common sum of 18 (which is shown here).

Secondly, 1 is in the middle, with a common sum of 14. Thirdly, 11 is in the middle, with a common sum of 22.

54. Cutting cake

Make one vertical cut that cuts the cake into left and right pieces. Make a second vertical cut that is perpendicular to the first cut. Make a third cut horizontally through the middle of the cake. The cake has now been cut into eight pieces.

55. Counting marbles

The possible answers are eleven less than multiples of 28 (e.g., 17, 45, 73, 101, etc.).

56. Cutting pizza

He should cut his piece into six equal pieces (each one of which is one-twelfth of the whole pizza), and give each brother one of these small pieces.

57. Arranging letters

There are two possible solutions.

A	B	C	D
C	D	A	B
D	C	B	A
B	A	D	C

A	B	C	D
D	C	B	A
B	A	D	C
C	D	A	B

58. A 3 × 3 magic square

The classic 3 × 3 magic square is shown here. For more regarding magic squares see 'Creating Magic Squares' in the Classroom Activities section of this book. There is also much more that can be studied on the Internet.

4	9	2
3	5	7
8	1	6

59. Dartboard

One possible solution is to hit 16 twice, and 17 four times.

60. Form tracing

One possible solution is shown here.

61. A string of digits

One possible solution is
9 - 8 + 76 - 5 + 4 + 3 + 21.
Another solution is 98 + 7 - 6 + 5 - 4 + 3 - 2 - 1.

62. Sums and differences

a) 24 and 17
b) 314 and 182

63. Halfway between

a) 65½
b) 655
c) 65,500
d) 5.6
e) 735
f) 9⅛
g) 7⅝
h) 5⁵⁄₁₂

64. Products, sums and differences

a) i) 8 and 5
    ii) 10 and 4
    iii) 20 and 2
b) i) 30 and 8
    ii) 80 and 3
    iii) 16 and 15
b) iv) 24 and 10
    v) 40 and 6
    vi) 48 and 5
c) 54 and 8
d) 62 and 11

65. Cricket score

Tumingham had 60 runs.

66. Fraction problems

a) 11 m 25 cm by 5 m 62½ cm (or 11.25 × 5.625 m)
b) All 8 legs add to 314 cm, so she needs a 3.6 m length of wood.

67. Coin puzzles

a) 13 50p coins (and 16 20p coins)
b) 18 20p and 32 10p coins

68. Age puzzles

a) Bill is 10.
b) Sue is 6 and Jeff is 23.
c) Tim is 21.
d) The youngest three are girls, and the oldest is a boy. Therefore, the youngest child has two sisters.

69. Digit arithmetic puzzles

a)
```
      5
      5
  +   5
 ─────
     15
```

c)
```
     1045
       45
  +  2867
 ──────
     3957
```

b)
```
      89
  +    9
 ─────
      98
```

70. Missing-digit multiplication

a)
```
       538
  ×     74
 ──────
      2152
  +  37660
 ──────
     39812
```

c)
```
      2386
  ×     22
 ──────
      4772
  +  47720
 ──────
     52492
```

b)
```
        59
  ×     73
 ──────
       177
  +   4130
 ──────
      4307
```

Class Seven Puzzles

71. Building chairs
It takes 3 days for 12 boys to build 12 chairs.

72. Connected circles
One solution is shown here:

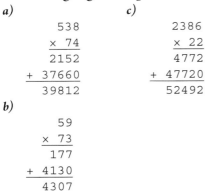

73. Hand washing
10p

74. A special number
The number is 47,347,347,347.

75. Four congruent pieces
Here is the solution:

76. A generous king
This is a preview of the idea of factorial. It is indeed surprising how quickly the number of coins grows. The twelfth person should receive $1 \times 2 \times 3 \times 4 \times 5 \times 6 \times 7 \times 8 \times 9 \times 10 \times 11 \times 12 = 479,001,600$ gold coins.

77. Connect-the-dots square
This requires 'out-of-the-box' thinking!

78. Siblings
a) She has 7 children (5 daughters and 2 sons).
b) There are 4 children (2 boys and 2 girls).

79. Stick puzzles
a)

b)

or

c)

d)

80. Sharing oranges

Stan should pay Bill 35p and pay Sara £2.45.

The reasoning is as follows: Everyone received 8 oranges. Therefore, Bill only gave Stan 1 orange, and Sara gave Stan 7 oranges. Since the ratio of the amount given by Sara and Bill is 7:1 (Sara gave 7 times as much as Stan), they should divide the money in that same ratio. Therefore, Bill gets ⅛ of the money and Sara gets ⅞ of the money (so Sara gets 7 times as much money as Stan).

81. Age puzzles

a) Tim is 7 and Frank is 13.
b) Jim is 8 and Mike is 20.
c) Brianna is 45 and Charlotte is 30.
d) Annie is 21 now.
e) Christine is 59 and Karen is 33.

82. Mixing apple juice and milk

Equal amounts of both! In the end, there is ⅘ of a cup of milk mixed into the apple juice jug, and ⅘ of a cup of apple juice mixed into the milk jug.

83. Products, sums and differences

84. Number riddles

a) 30 and 7   *c)* 14 and 15
b) 42 and 5   *d)* 35 and 6

a) 125 and 85   *d)* 17 and 6
b) 49, 77, 91   *e)* 16 and 19
c) 23 and 25

85. Coin puzzles

a) 15 10p coins
b) i) 26 10p, 14 50p coins
    ii) 8 10p, 24 20p, 8 50p coins
    iii) 20 10p, 8 20p, 12 50p coins

86. Digit arithmetic puzzles

a)
```
      23
      23
      23
   +  23
      92
```

b)
```
      9567
   +  1085
     10652
```

c)
```
     62932
   − 58206
      4726
```

87. Missing-digits

a)
```
        23
   7 ‾1‾6‾1
   −  14
       21
   −   21
        0
```

b)
```
          38
   50 ‾1‾9‾0‾0
    −  150
       400
    −  400
         0
```

c)
```
       573
    ×  219
      5157
      5730
   + 114600
    125487
```

88. A long line

We need to add 1+2+3+4+…+199. One easy way to do this is to add them in pairs: (1+199) + (2+198) + (3+197) +…We then notice that each pair adds to 200, and that there are 99 pairs, with the number 100 having no partner. Therefore, the total sum is 200 × 99 + 100, which is 19,900 metres – almost 20 km.

89. Pieces on a chessboard

One solution is shown here:

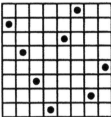

90. Chessboard squares

64 squares are 1 by 1,
49 squares are 2 by 2,
36 squares are 3 by 3,
25 squares are 4 by 4,
16 squares are 5 by 5,
9 squares are 6 by 6,
4 squares are 7 by 7,
1 square is 8 by 8.
Altogether, we get a total of 204 squares.

91. The race

The order is: Ed, Abe, Dan, Charles, Ben.

92. Two jugs

It appears that there are two solutions to each case. You may either pour each time from the large jug into the small one, or each time from the small one into the large one. It is interesting to see that if you simply keep pouring from one into the other, all of the numbers will eventually appear. Also, if you switch which jug is pouring into which, the numbers appear in reverse order. Additional solutions may be found that are a mix of these two approaches.

Pouring from the small (4 ℓ) into the large jug (9 ℓ)
(otherwise known as the hard way to get to 5 ℓ)
8 litres: Fill the small jug twice and pour it into the large one. This gives you 8 ℓ in the large jug.
3 litres: Now refill the small jug and pour it into the large one until it is full (1 ℓ will fit). This leaves 3 ℓ in the small jug.
7 litres: Empty the large jug, and then pour the 3 ℓ from the small jug into the large one. Refill the small jug and pour the small jug into the large jug (adding 4 ℓ). You now have 7 ℓ in the large jug.
2 litres: Now refill the small jug and pour it into the large one until it is full (2 ℓ will fit). This leaves 2 ℓ in the small jug.
6 litres: Empty the large jug, and then pour the 2 ℓ from the small jug into the large one. Refill the small jug and pour the small jug into the large jug (adding 4 ℓ). You now have 6 ℓ in the large jug.
1 litre: Now refill the small jug and pour it into the large one until it is full (3 ℓ will fit). This leaves 1 ℓ in the small jug.
5 litres: Empty the large jug, and then pour the 1 ℓ from the small jug into the large one. Refill the small jug and pour the small jug into the large jug (adding 4 ℓ). You now have 5 ℓ in the large jug.

Pouring from the large (9 ℓ) into the small jug (4 ℓ)
(otherwise known as the hard way to get to 8 ℓ)
5 litres: Fill the large jug and pour it into the small jug until it is full. This leaves 5 ℓ in the large jug.

1 litre: Empty the small jug and pour the large jug into the small jug (subtracting 4 ℓ). You now have 1 ℓ in the large jug.

6 litres: Empty the small jug, and then pour the 1 ℓ from the large jug into the small one. Now refill the large jug and pour it into the small one until it is full (3 ℓ will fit). This leaves 6 ℓ in the large jug.

2 litres: Empty the small jug, and pour the large jug into the small jug (subtracting 4 ℓ). You now have 2 ℓ in the large jug.

7 litres: Empty the small jug, and then pour the 2 ℓ from the large jug into the small one. Now refill the large jug and pour it into the small one until it is full (2 ℓ will fit). This leaves 7 ℓ in the large jug.

3 litres: Empty the small jug and pour the large jug into the small jug (subtracting 4 ℓ). You now have 3 ℓ in the large jug.

8 litres: Empty the small jug and then pour the 3 ℓ from the large jug into the small one. Now refill the large jug and pour it into the small one until it is full (1 ℓ will fit). This leaves 8 ℓ in the large jug.

93. More pets

In total, they have 32 pets. One possible way to arrive at the solution is to realise that (because of the second and third sentences) Charlie has 7 more pets than Ben. We also know that Ben and Charlie have 15 pets combined, so we can figure out (with a bit of thinking) that Ben must have 4 pets, and Charlie must have 11 pets. The rest is easy.

94. Concert tickets

1600 section B tickets and 2900 section A tickets.

95. The money wizard

Peggy started with £5.25.

96. Wishful banking

Since each month we are multiplying by two, we can express the relationship between the number of months and the balance as $£ = 0.25 \times 2^m$, where £ is the balance and m is the number of months. An equivalent, and more convenient formula is $£ = 2^{m-2}$. Either way, the answers work out to:

After one year: £1024

After two years: £4,194,304

After five years: £288,230,376,151,711,744 (288 quadrillion pounds)

97. Tear and stack

After 1 tear we have 2 sheets, after 2 tears we have 4 sheets, after 3 tears we have 8 sheets, after 4 tears we have 16 sheets, etc. We can see that the number of sheets (2, 4, 8, 16, etc.) is always a power of two, which can be expressed by the formula $S = 2^n$, where S is the number of sheets, and n is the number of times that the stack has been torn and stacked. Putting in 42 for n, gives us 2^{42}, which can be written as $2^2 \times 2^{10} \times 2^{10} \times 2^{10} \times 2^{10}$, and since $2^{10} \approx 1000$, we can say that $2^{42} \approx 4,000,000,000,000$.

Since a ream (500 sheets) is 4.5 cm thick (or 1000 sheets is 9 cm thick) each sheet is 0.009 cm thick. We then can calculate that the stack is about 36,000,000,000 cm, or 360,000 km high.

The exact answer is 395,824 km high, which is a bit more than the distance to the moon (384,000 km)!

98. A row of houses

Facts Nos. 1, 2, 6, 10, 15 tell us that the South African lives in the left-most house (house No. 1), and, most importantly, that his house must be yellow. We now know that the red house must be either house No. 3 or house No. 5. If we try assigning house No. 5 to red, and follow all of the other facts, we end up with a contradiction, so we know that house No. 3 must be red. From this point onwards there is a fair bit of trial and error. But eventually we get our answer: The South African drinks water, and the Nepali has a zebra.

99. Towers of Hanoi

For a stack of 2 disks it takes 3 moves; 3 disks take 7 moves; 4 disks take 15 moves; 5 disks take 31 moves, etc. We can base each answer on the previous answer. For example, with 4 disks, we know that it takes 7 moves to transfer the top three disks to another peg, then one move to move the largest disk to the empty peg, and finally, 7 more moves to get the stack of three disks back on top of the largest disk. Therefore, moving the whole stack of 4 disks takes 7+1+7 = 15 moves. Similarly, moving 5 disks would take 15+1+15 = 31 moves.

Now we can notice that all the number of moves (3, 7, 15, 31, etc.) are one less than a power of two (4, 8, 16, 32, etc.). From this, we can make a formula that calculates the number of moves needed (M) based on the number of disks (D). The formula is:

$$M = 2^D - 1.$$

Therefore, the number of moves needed to move an entire stack of 64 disks is $2^{64} - 1$. This can be estimated by ignoring the minus 1, and realising that

$$2^{64} = 2^4 \times 2^{10} \times 2^{10} \times 2^{10} \times 2^{10} \times 2^{10}.$$

And since $2^4 = 16$ and $2^{10} = 1024$ (which is approximately 1000) we can say that $2^{64} \approx 16,000,000,000,000,000,000$. This is approximately the total number of moves needed to move the whole stack of 64 disks. It is also the total number of seconds needed to move the whole stack, given that each move takes one second.

How many years is this? We first calculate the number of seconds in a year. There are 60 seconds in a minute, $60 \times 60 = 3600$ seconds in an hour, $3600 \times 24 = 86,400$ seconds in day, and, finally, $86,400 \times 365 = 31,536,000$ seconds in a year, which we can approximate as 32,000,000. The number of years is therefore $16,000,000,000,000,000,000 \div 32,000,000$, which, when looked at as a fraction, reduces nicely to $1,000,000,000,000 \div 2$, which equals 500,000,000,000 years, or half a trillion years. The exact number of years is 584,942,417,335, which shows that our quick estimate is quite accurate.

Class Eight Puzzles

100. Siblings

There are 13 children in the family (10 girls and 3 boys).

101. Socks in the dark

a) You must pull out at least 5 (single) socks.
b) You must pull out at least 7 (single) socks.
c) You must pull out at least 9 (single) socks.

102. Brick laying

A single brick is 15 by $22\frac{1}{2}$ cm.

103. Jill's bike ride

The distance from the second sign to Manson is $\frac{1}{5}$ of the whole distance (Brownsville to Manson). Therefore, the second sign to Gilpin is $\frac{2}{5}$ of the whole distance, and the remaining distance (Brownsville to Gilpin) is $\frac{2}{5}$ of the whole distance. Since the distance from the first sign to Gilpin is twice as far as the distance from the first sign to Brownsville, the first sign must be $\frac{1}{3}$ of the way from Brownsville to Gilpin. And since we just said that Brownsville to Gilpin is $\frac{2}{5}$ of the whole trip, we now know that Brownsville to the first sign must be $\frac{2}{15}$ ($= \frac{1}{3} \times \frac{2}{5}$) of the whole trip, and the distance from the first sign to Gilpin must be $\frac{4}{15}$ of the whole trip. Therefore, the distance between the two signs must be $\frac{2}{3}$ ($= \frac{2}{5} + \frac{4}{15}$) of the distance of the whole trip, or, stated in reverse, the distance of the whole trip must be $\frac{3}{2}$ of the distance between the signs, which we know is 36 km. So the length of the whole trip is $\frac{3}{2} \times 36$ or 54 km.

104. Divisibility and powers

a) no	***d)*** no	***g)*** no
b) yes	***e)*** yes	***h)*** yes
c) no	***f)*** yes	***i)*** no

105. Kate's grandfather

He was 89 years old in 1981. (In 1936 he was $\sqrt{1936} = 44$.)

106. Stick puzzles

a)

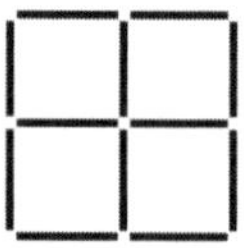

c)

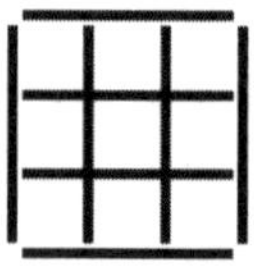

b)

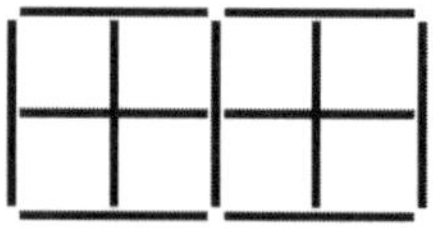

107. Digit arithmetic puzzles

a)

```
  4950
+ 4990
  9940
```

b)

```
  1090
-  999
    91
```

c)

```
   764
+  325
  1089
```

108. Three schools

One way to do it is to work with ratios. We can quickly see that the ratio of the number of students of Bob's school to Alex's school is 2:1. And, since one-quarter the number of students at Bob's school is equal to one-third the number of students at Chris's school, then that ratio must be 4:3. Therefore, the ratio of the three schools is 4:3:2, which means that Bob's school is $\frac{4}{9}$ of the total, Alex's school is $\frac{3}{9}$ of the total, and Chris's school is $\frac{2}{9}$ of the total. This leads to our desired result that the number of students at the three schools is 236, 177, and 118.

109. Arranging points

Simply draw a five-pointed star. Five of the points fall on the vertices of the star, and five fall on the inner (inscribed) pentagon.

110. Coin puzzles

a) 24 20p , 6 50p coins
b) 18 10p, 12 50p coins
c) 12 10p, 8 20p, 10 50p coins
d) 15 10p , 4 20p, 11 50p coins

111. Tennis club

We are looking for the smallest number *(x)* that is divisible by all of the numbers 1 to 8 (that is, the numbers 1 to 8 must be factors of *x*). The smallest such number has the prime factorisation $2^3 \times 3 \times 5 \times 7$, which is 840. They will all play again after 840 days.

112. Number riddles

a) 7 and 8
b) 5 and 16
c) A croissant costs £2.10
d) Mary has £14.50.
e) Frank weighs 42 kg.
f) 8½ and 16
g) 6⅔ and 25⅓
h) 12 and 23, or –12 and –23

113. Age puzzles

a) Cathy is 22.
b) Fred is 9; Andy is 13.
c) Bill is 17.
d) Karen is 16.
e) Lacy, Stacy and Tracy may be 3, 4, 20; or 4, 6, 10; or 5, 8, 6; or 6, 10, 4.

114. Shovelling snow

a) One hour and 20 minutes.
b) The area of this square is 100 times greater than the original square. Therefore, the time must be 100 times as much. The answer is 2000 minutes, or 1 day, 9 hours, 20 minutes (assuming she doesn't have a break).

115. Missing digits

a)
```
      113
    × 133
      339
     3390
 +  11300
    15029
```

b)
```
     1475
    × 677
    10325
   103250
 + 885000
   998575
```

c)
```
        90809
  12 1089708
   -  108
         97
       - 96
        108
      - 108
          0
```

116. Six 6s

There are many possible solutions for each one.

$1 = 666 \div 666$

$2 = \dfrac{6}{\frac{6+6}{6} + \frac{6}{6}}$

$3 = \dfrac{6}{6} + \dfrac{6}{6} + \dfrac{6}{6}$

$4 = \dfrac{6+6}{6} + \dfrac{6+6}{6}$

$5 = \dfrac{6+6+6+6+6}{6}$

$6 = \dfrac{66 - 66}{6} + 6$

$7 = \dfrac{6-6}{6} + \dfrac{6}{6} + 6$

$8 = \dfrac{66 - 6 - 6 - 6}{6}$

$9 = \dfrac{66 - 6}{6} - \dfrac{6}{6}$

$10 = \dfrac{66 - 6}{6} + 6 - 6$

117. Eight 8s

Some possible solutions are:

$(8888 - 888) \div 8$

$888 + 8(8 + 8) - 8 - 8$

$888 + 88 + 8 + 8 + 8$

$8[8(8 + 8) - (8 + 8 + 8) \div 8]$

$((88 - 8) \div 8)^{((8+8+8) \div 8)}$

118. Plane tickets

27 first class seats were sold.

119. A batch of biscuits

120 biscuits were in the original batch.

120. Connect-the-dot squares

There are 9 squares with sides of length 1,
4 squares with sides of length 2,
1 square with a side of length 3,
4 squares (diamonds) with sides of length $\sqrt{2}$,
and 2 (tilted) squares with sides of length $\sqrt{5}$.
Therefore, the total number of squares is 20.

121. A changing choir

If the choir is 72% women, then the ratio of men to women must be 28:72, which is 7:18. Since we know the number of men is 21, we can determine the number of women by setting up this proportion: $7 : 18 = 21 : x$. Solving this yields $x = 54$, so 25 new women must join.

122. The locker puzzle

The key to this problem is that a locker changes for each factor of its assigned number (for instance, locker No. 15 changes on 1, 3, 5, 15). The real question becomes: which numbers have an odd number of factors? The answer to this is that in order to have an odd number of factors, a number must be a perfect square. Therefore, only the lockers with numbers that are perfect squares will be left open, namely: 1, 4, 9, 16, 25, 36, 49, 64, 81, 100, 121, 144, 169, 196, 225, 256, 289.

123. Shaking hands

Perhaps it is best to imagine one person at a time entering a room, and shaking hands with each of the people already in the room. The second person shakes hands once upon entering, the third person shakes hands twice upon entering, the fourth person three times, etc. The question then becomes: 'What does n need to be such that the sum of the numbers from 1 to n will equal 120?' After some trial and error, or perhaps working with Gauss's formula, we see that n must be 15, which means that 16 people are required in order to have 120 handshakes. We can check our answer by realising that all 16 people, in the end, will shake hands 15 times. If we multiply 15 × 16, we get 240, but we divide by 2 (to get 120 handshakes) because otherwise each handshake would be counted twice.

124. Inner tube inversion

I have promised certain people that I'd never tell the answer to this imagination puzzle! Of course, you could try it with a real inner tube – but that might be considered cheating!

125. Slicing a triangle

Shown here is one way to divide an equilateral triangle into 4, 6, 3 and 2 congruent pieces.

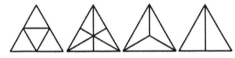

It should also be noted that any right triangle can be divided into four congruent pieces, as shown here.

By nesting these arrangements in various ways, we can also get 8, 12, 16, 24, 32, etc., congruent pieces. These numbers come from these sequences:

4^n (which gives us 1, 4, 16, 64 ...)
2×4^n (which gives us 2, 8, 32 ...)
3×4^n (which gives us 3, 12, 48 ...)
6×4^n (which gives us 6, 24, 96...)
Notice that 9, 18, 36, etc., congruent pieces are not possible.

126. Grains of rice

a) The number of grains on the last square is 2^{63}. The number of grains on the whole board is $2^{64}-1 = 18,446,744,073,709,551,615$.

b) Rounding the number of grains to 18,400,000,000,000,000,000 and dividing by 400,000 gives us approximately 46,000,000,000,000 (46 trillion) sacks of rice. Since each sack is 50 cm long, the length of the line of sacks works out to be about 2,300,000,000,000,000 cm, which is 23,000,000,000 km, which is about 156 times further than the distance to the sun!

c) If there are 400 grains of rice in 15 mℓ there are about 26,667 in 1 ℓ (for simplicity let's say about 25,000 grains). There are 1000 ℓ in one cubic metre, so a cubic metre will contain about 25,000,000 grains. A cubic km $(1000 \times 1000 \times 1000 \text{ m})$ will contain about 25,000,000,000,000,000. Dividing the total number of grains by this number gives about 740 cubic kilometres!

Upper School Puzzles

Geometric puzzles

127. Slicing a hexagon

128. The snail's journey
We can imagine that we could 'unwind' the path he took, and we would get a right triangle where the base would be 16.8 (which is 7×24), and the height would be 7. The hypotenuse of this triangle is indeed the path he travelled, which turns out to be 18.2 m.

129. Making a square
It is helpful here to realise that the area of the square must be 5, so the length of the side of the square must be $\sqrt{5}$. The question then becomes, 'How can we make a line of length ?' Well, this is the length of the hypotenuse of a right triangle that has legs of length 2 and 1. Two possible solutions are shown here.

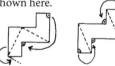

130. A shaded region
Let x be the vertical height of the left edge of the shaded region, and let y be the length of the slanted top of the shaded region. Using similar triangles, we can set up the ratio $5 : x = 13 : 8$,

which yields an x value equal to $^{40}/_{13} \approx 3.08$. Using the Pythagorean theorem allows us to calculate that y is approximately 9.39. We can then calculate that the area of the shaded region is approximately 44.3, and the perimeter is approximately 28.5.

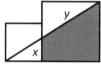

131. Connected circles
The key is to construct a right triangle (as shown here) where the horizontal leg has a length equal to the sum of the circles' radii, and the vertical leg has a length equal to the difference of the circles' radii. The legs are therefore 24 and 10. By using the Pythagorean theorem, or recognising that these numbers are in a Pythagorean triple ratio (5-12-13), we can determine that the line connecting the circles' centres has a length of 26.

132. Nested polyhedra
If we assign the length of the cube's edge equal to 1, then the tetrahedron has an edge of length $\sqrt{2}$, and the octahedron has an edge of length $\frac{\sqrt{2}}{2}$. The formula for the volume of a tetrahedron is $V = \frac{\sqrt{2}}{12} \times E^3$, and the formula for the volume of an octahedron is $V = \frac{\sqrt{2}}{3} \times E^3$. (You should derive these two formulas for yourself!) Plugging in the edge lengths into their respective formulas, gives us that the tetrahedron's volume is $^1/_3$, and the octahedron's volume is $^1/_6$. Therefore, the ratio of the volumes

of the nested polyhedra (as given in the drawing) is:
Cube : Tetrahedron : Octahedron = 6:2:1.

133. Paths on a globe

There are infinitely many starting places for which this is possible – or 'infinity times infinity plus one'. The North Pole is one such place. There are no other places in the northern hemisphere.

However, in the southern hemisphere you could start at a place (very close to the South Pole), such that the second leg of your trip (heading east) exactly circumnavigates a latitude line, which happens to be exactly 1 km long. In that case, the last leg of your trip (heading north) retraces in reverse the first leg of your trip (heading south). You could have started your journey from any point that is 1 km to the north of that latitude line.

Furthermore, additional starting places are possible even closer to the South Pole. For example, the 1-km long eastward leg of the trip could have circled *twice* around a half-km long latitudinal line. In fact, this would work as long as we choose a length (in km) for the latitudinal line that is equal to the reciprocal of a whole number ($\frac{1}{3}$, $\frac{1}{4}$, $\frac{1}{5}$, ...). If we choose such a length for a latitudinal line, then we will we go around this latitudinal line (which is really a circle) a number of times in order to complete the 1-km long eastward leg of the trip.

Now we see that there are an infinite number of latitude lines to use, and each one has an infinite number of points from which the journey could start.

Thus, our answer is, infinity times infinity, plus one (the North Pole).

134. Four points

Imagine a plane, λ, passing through three of the points, and a plane, μ, parallel to λ, but passing through the fourth point. One plane that is equidistant from all four points is halfway between planes λ and μ. Since λ could have been chosen passing through any three of the four points, there are four such planes.

The second type of equidistant plane has two of the points on one side of it, and two on the other side. Call the four points W, X, Y, Z. Through the line WX, there are infinitely many planes (a pencil of planes), and through YZ there are infinitely many planes. Let plane ξ be the (unique) plane passing through WX that is parallel to the line YZ, and plane π be the (unique) plane passing through YZ that is parallel to the line WX. Plane π and ξ must be parallel to each other. Halfway between π and ξ lies a plane that is equidistant to all four given points.

Of course, there are three ways that we could have grouped the four points (WX and YZ being one of the three ways). Therefore, for this second type, there are three planes that are equally far from all four points, where two points are on one side of the plane and two are on the other. In total, there are seven planes that are equidistant from the four given points.

135. Three vertical lines

Draw a horizontal line through the top of the line marked originally as x. Using similar triangles we get $a : b = 10 : 15 = 2 : 3$, and from the triangle proportionality theorem we know that $a : b = y : x$. Therefore, $y : x = 2 : 3$. From this, we can say that x is ⅗ of the whole line that has a length of 10. Thus, $x = 6$.

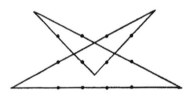

136. Connecting twelve dots

137. Leonardo da Vinci's lunes

A generalised statement of the Pythagorean theorem tells us that the area of the largest semi-circle must equal the sum of the areas of the two smaller semi-circles. After some more work, we can conclude (surprisingly!) that the sum of the areas of the two lunes equals the area of the right triangle, which is ½ab.

138. Pythagorean quadruples

a) 17

b) $d^2 = a^2 + b^2 + c^2$

c) One possible method is to rewrite the formula as $a^2 + b^2 = d^2 - c^2$ and then as $a^2 + b^2 = (d - c)(d + c)$.

Now, choose any Pythagorean triple (not necessarily reduced), and assign a and b to the legs of that triple, and let x be the hypotenuse of that triple. This means that $a^2 + b^2 = x^2$ and that $x^2 = (d - c)(d + c)$. Now find two numbers (either both odd if x^2 is odd, or both even if x^2 is even) whose product is equal to x^2. Then c will be half the distance between the two numbers, and d will the average of the two numbers.

For example, choosing the Pythagorean triple 12, 16, 20, gives us $a = 12$, $b = 16$, $x = 20$. Then x^2 is 400. Choosing 8 and 50 as the two numbers that multiply to 400, gives us $d - c = 8$ and $d + c = 50$. This leads to $c = 21$, and $d = 29$ for a Pythagorean quadruple $(12, 16, 21, 29)$. Choosing differently from 8 and 50 would have yielded the quadruples $(12, 16, 99, 101)$, $(12, 16, 15, 25)$, and $(12, 16, 48, 52)$, which reduces to $(3, 4, 12, 13)$.

Some other Pythagorean quadruples are: $(1, 2, 2, 3)$; $(2, 3, 6, 7)$; $(4, 4, 7, 9)$; $(9, 12, 20, 25)$; $(9, 12, 112, 113)$.

139. Squares and circles

The smaller square has a length of ⅗. The radii are ³⁹⁄₃₂₀ and ¹⁄₁₆.

These solutions can be arrived at in the following way. The top drawing shows how we can find the dimensions of the smaller square.

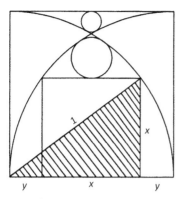

We then get the two equations:

$x + 2y = 1$

$1^2 = x^2 + (x + y)^2$

Solving these two equations leads to the answer $x = \frac{3}{5}$.

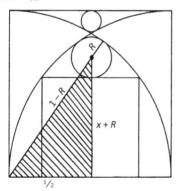

The drawing above is based on the fact that a line drawn from the point of tangency (of the larger circle and the quarter-arc) to the bottom-left corner of the larger square must pass through the centre of the larger circle. This leads to the equation:

$(1 - R)^2 = (\frac{1}{2})^2 + (x + R)^2$

Knowing that x (the length of the smaller square) is equal to $\frac{3}{5}$ leads to an answer of $R = \frac{39}{320}$.

The third drawing (below) leads to the equation:

$(1 + r)^2 = (\frac{1}{2})^2 + (1 - r)^2$

and the answer of $r = \frac{1}{16}$.

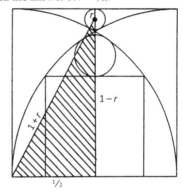

140. Three shadows

This is a three-dimensional geometry problem, and a good preparation for matrix algebra and vector physics problems. All you really need to solve this problem is the Pythagorean theorem.

The business about shadows is really a long way around saying the following: the rectangular block can describe a coordinate system, and that the length given on each face can be thought of as the result of the Pythagorean theorem for the 2 dimensions on that face. If we imagine coordinates in x, y and z at mutually orthogonal directions, then face A could be the x-z plane, B could be the x-y plane, and C the y-z plane. The Pythagorean theorem states: $a^2 + b^2 = c^2$, where a is the change in coordinate length in one direction, b the change in length in the orthogonal direction, and c the total length in that plane.

Therefore, we can write:

Face A $\quad \Delta x^2 \quad\quad + \Delta z^2 \quad = 25 \quad$ equation (1)
Face B $\quad \Delta x^2 + \Delta y^2 \quad\quad = 36 \quad\quad\quad (2)$
Face C $\quad\quad\quad \Delta y^2 + \Delta z^2 \quad = 49 \quad\quad\quad (3)$

One way to solve this is as follows:

$$\Delta x^2 \quad\quad + \Delta z^2 \;=\; 25$$
$$\Delta x^2 + \Delta y^2 \quad\quad = \; 36$$
$$\underline{\Delta y^2 + \Delta z^2 \;=\; 49}$$
$$\underline{-\Delta y^2 + \Delta z^2 \;=\; -11 \quad \text{subtracting } (2) \text{ from } (1)}$$
$$\Delta y^2 + \Delta z^2 \;=\; 49$$
$$\underline{}$$
$$2\,\Delta z^2 \;=\; 38 \quad \text{adding the 2 equations above}$$
$$\Delta z^2 \;=\; 19 \quad \text{result}$$

It then follows that:

$$\Delta x^2 = 6 \;;\; \Delta y^2 = 30 \;;\; \Delta z^2 = 19$$

Therefore, the overall length of the rod is
$$r = \sqrt{\Delta x^2 + \Delta y^2 + \Delta z^2}$$
$$= \sqrt{6 + 30 + 19} \;=\; \sqrt{55} \text{ cm.}$$

141. Four intersecting circles

Here are some key steps:

$\angle AEB = 30°$

Length $AB =$ $2\sin(15°)$, which is $\frac{\sqrt{6} - \sqrt{2}}{2}$.

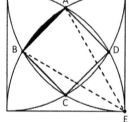

The area of $\triangle ABE = \frac{1}{4}$.

The area of the circular segment ABE (which is pie-shaped and is one-twelfth of the whole circle) is $^\pi/_{12}$.

The area of the (thin shaded) section
$$AB = \frac{\pi}{12} - \frac{1}{4} = \frac{\pi - 3}{12}.$$

Area of square $ABCD = 2 - \sqrt{3}$.

The central region is the sum of the square $ABCD$ and the four (thin shaded) circular sections:

$$4\left(\frac{\pi - 3}{12}\right) + 2 - \sqrt{3} \;\to\; \tfrac{1}{3}\pi - \sqrt{3} + 1 \approx 0.315$$

Algebraic puzzles

142. Four numbers in a square

1	2
1	6

143. Age puzzles

a) Interestingly, it doesn't matter how old they were in the beginning. Given P_1 and S_1 as their initial ages, and P_2 and S_2 as their ages later, we have the following (we want to find x):

$$S_1 = 11P_1; \;\; P_2 = 2P_1; \;\; S_2 = S_1 + P_1$$

The desired question can be framed as
$$S_2 = xP_2$$

Substituting gives us $S_1 + P_1 = x(2P_1)$ —>
$$11P_1 + P_1 = x(2P_1) \;\text{—>}$$
$$12P_1 = 2P_1 x \text{ —> } 12 = 2x \text{ —> } x = 6$$

Therefore, Sue will be 6 times older than Paul.

b) If x is the length of Diophantus's life, and y is the length of his son's life, then we get the equations:

$$x = \tfrac{1}{6}x + \tfrac{1}{12}x + \tfrac{1}{7}x + 5 + y + 4 \text{ and } y = \tfrac{1}{2}x$$

Solving for x tells us that Diophantus lived 84 years.

144. Brothers and sisters

There are 13 children in the family (4 girls and 9 boys).

145. A herd of cows

This lends itself nicely to an algebraic equation, where x stands for the number of cows in the herd:

$x = \frac{1}{5}x + \frac{1}{3}x + 2\left(\frac{1}{3}x - \frac{1}{5}x\right) + 18.$

Solving for x, tells us that there are 90 cows in the herd.

146. Two-digit numbers

a) The number is 18.

b) Surprisingly, it turns out that each number simply needs to be such that one digit is twice the other digit. The possible answers are 12 & 21, 24 & 42, 36 & 63, and 48 & 84.

c) The numbers are 41 and 51.

147. House painting

Perhaps it helps to invert the rates – in other words, instead of thinking of someone painting a house at a rate of 6 hours per 1 house, we express the same thing as $\frac{1}{6}$ house per hour. The three rates are then $\frac{1}{6}$ house per hour, $\frac{1}{4}$ house per hour, and $\frac{1}{3}$ house per hour. We see then that the combined rate is $\left(\frac{1}{6} + \frac{1}{4} + \frac{1}{3}\right) = \frac{3}{4}$ house per hour, which is also $\frac{4}{3}$ hour per house.

Therefore, it should take 1 hour and 20 minutes to paint the house if they work together.

148. Guessing one number

We simply translate the teacher's instructions: 'Choose any number. Add 7. Multiply by 3. Subtract the original number.' into the following algebraic expression: $3(x + 7) - x$, which simplifies to: $2x + 21$. In order to get x (the student's original number), we just subtract 21 from the student's final result, and then divide by 2.

149. Guessing two numbers

Look at the first part of the teacher's instructions:

'Choose any two numbers. The third number is what you get when you add together your first two numbers. The fourth number is the second and third numbers added together. The fifth number is equal to third and fourth numbers added together.'

The student's list of numbers can be represented algebraically as:

x (the first number)
y (the second number)
$x + y$ (the third number)
$x + 2y$ (the fourth number)
$2x + 3y$ (the fifth number)

The sum of these five numbers is $5x + 7y$.

The next part of the teacher's instructions is:

'Now, carefully add up all five numbers. Subtract from this sum twice your second number. Tell me your result.'

This translates into $(5x + 7y) - 2y$, which simplifies to $5x + 5y$.

We now know that the student's first result is: $R_1 = 5x + 5y$.

Now look at the final part of the teacher's instructions:

'Take the answer that you just gave me and subtract from it, ten times your first number. Tell me what number you now have.'

This translates into $(5x + 5y) - 10x$, which simplifies to $5y - 5x$.

We now know that the student's second result is: $R_2 = 5y - 5x$.

So here is the teacher's trick:

To get the student's second number (y in the original list), simply add the two results ($R_1 + R_2$), which gives us $10y$, and then divide by 10.

To get the student's first number (x in the original list), simply subtract the two results ($R_1 - R_2$), which gives us $10x$, and then divide by 10.

Try a couple of examples yourself to see how it works.

150. Guessing three numbers

Given x, y and z as the three numbers, the teacher's instructions simply translate to:
$$10\left(5(2x+5)+y-4\right)+3+z.$$

The student's final result (R) is then equal to the above expression, which simplifies to:
$$R = 100x + 10y + z + 213$$

The teacher simply takes the student's result (R), and subtracts 213, which gives the student's three original digits, x, y and z.

151. Average speeds

We can derive two equations from the given information:
$$75\left(T - \tfrac{1}{30}\right) = D \text{ and } 65\left(T + \tfrac{1}{30}\right) = D,$$

where T is the amount of time it would take to be exactly on time, D is the distance from her house to work, and $\tfrac{1}{30}$ of an hour is used in place of 2 minutes. Solving these two equations gives us $T = \tfrac{7}{15}$ hour, or 28 minutes.

This means that when she drives 65 km/h, it takes $\tfrac{7}{15} + \tfrac{1}{30} = \tfrac{1}{2}$ hour to get to work.

Therefore, $D = 65 \times 1/2 = 32\tfrac{1}{2}$ km.

152. More average speed

We can derive a general formula for these problems, where D is the distance between the home and the office, the rates back and forth are R_1 and R_2, and the average rate for the whole trip is R_A.

The total distance is $2D$, and the total time is $\tfrac{D}{R_1} + \tfrac{D}{R_2}$.

Therefore, $R_A = \dfrac{\text{total distance}}{\text{total time}} = \dfrac{2D}{\frac{D}{R_1} + \frac{D}{R_2}}$.

With further work, this simplifies to
$$\frac{1}{R_A} = \frac{1}{2}\left(\frac{1}{R_1} + \frac{1}{R_2}\right).$$

In other words, the average rate for the whole trip is the harmonic mean of the rates back and forth. We can now use this formula to solve the problems.

a) Impossible. He would have to go 'infinitely fast'. As an explanation, imagine that the distance to the office is 20 miles, so that the whole trip would be 40 miles. In order to average 20 mph for the whole trip, he would have to cover the full 40 miles in 2 hours. However, he already used the whole 2 hours just to get to the office. This leaves him no time to get back.

b) 30 mph, which is what many people think the answer to the first problem is.

c) 90 mph.

d) Impossible.

153. The leopard and the dog

We know that if the dog runs toward the leopard, it covers $\tfrac{3}{8}$ of the bridge in the time it takes for the leopard to arrive at the start of the bridge. If the dog were to run the other way, then at the instant that the dog had run another ⅜ of the distance along the bridge, the leopard would be just at the start of the bridge. The dog would then be running the remaining ¼ of the bridge in the time the leopard covers the whole bridge. The leopard therefore must be going 4 times faster than the dog, which is 60 km/h.

154. Crossing ripples

Because the man is travelling at a constant rate, and the distances that he travelled before crossing the ripple are equal (both are 12 m), we know that the size of the circular ripple when he crossed it the second time must be twice what it was when he crossed it the first time. With the diagrams shown here, A is the position of the boat when the fish jumped, C is where the fish jumped, B is the place where the boat first crossed the ripple, and D is the second place where the boat crossed the ripple.

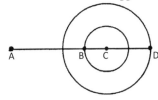

We know that AB and BD are both 12 m. Because BD is 12 m and the three segments are equal, we can label each of them as 4.

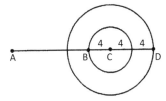

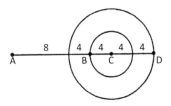

And then we know that because AB is 12 m, its two segments must be 8 and 4. Therefore, at the beginning, the distance from the boat to the fish (AC) must have been 16 m.

155. Sums of multiples

In this case, we are dealing with three series:

Multiples of three: $3 + 6 + 9 + … + 999$; sum $(\Sigma) = 166{,}833$

Multiples of five: $5 + 10 + 15 + … + 1000$; $\Sigma = 100{,}500$

Multiples of fifteen: $15 + 30 + 45 + … + 990$; $\Sigma = 33{,}165$

To get our answer we add the number of multiples of three to the number of multiples of five. However, we have just counted some of the numbers (the multiples of 15) twice. So we subtract the number of multiples of 15.

$166{,}833 + 100{,}500 - 33{,}165 = 234{,}168.$

156. Clock hands

One way to approach this problem is by imagining that at exactly 4:00 a race begins where the minute hand sets off to catch up with the hour hand. Since there are 60 tick marks on the clock, we can set our standard of measurement to one 'tick mark', and say that the minute hand is moving at a rate of 60 ticks/h and the hour hand is moving at a rate of 5 ticks/h. The minute hand is therefore catching up at a rate of 55 ticks/h. Given that the minute hand started out 20 tick marks behind the hour hand, the amount of time for the minute hand to catch up is 20 ticks ÷ 55 ticks/h, which is $^4/_{11}$ of an hour, or $21^9/_{11}$ minutes. Therefore, the hands are exactly together at $4:21^9/_{11}$, which is 21 minutes $49^1/_{11}$ seconds (or ≈ 49.1 seconds) after 4 o'clock.

157. The itinerant monk

This problem is the same as the following scenario: Two monks start hiking at the same time – one from the bottom of the mountain going uphill, and the other from the top going downhill. What time do they meet?

As the original problem states, the trail is 6 km long, they leave at 7 am, and their speeds are in a 2:5 ratio. Looked at in this way, we can say that at the moment they meet, one monk has covered $^5/_7$ of the distance, and the other has covered $^2/_7$ of the distance. Therefore, they meet $^5/_7 \times 6 \approx 4.29$ km from the temple.

158. A shepherd's flock

Given that the number of sheep is P,
the first son gets $1 + \frac{P-1}{7}$ sheep, which simplifies to $\frac{P+6}{7}$, and
the second son gets $2 + \frac{\frac{P+6}{7} - 2}{7}$ sheep, which simplifies to $\frac{6P+78}{49}$.

Since the first two sons received an equal number of sheep, we set $\frac{P+6}{7} = \frac{6P+78}{49}$.

Solving this equation tells us that the number of sheep in the original flock (P) is 36. Now that we know the value of P, we know that each son receives 6 sheep, and that there are 6 sons.

159. The horrific age puzzle

Alex is 5, Beth is 14, Craig is 9. An explanation of this solution follows.

We can set up equations that translate phrase by phrase. A, B and C are the current ages of the people, and t_n represents a number of years into the future. Shown below, are 12 equations with 12 variables.

Eleven years from now, Alex will be four times as old as Craig was

$$A + 11 = 4(C + t_1) \tag{1}$$

when Beth was three times as old as Alex was two years ago.

$$B + t_1 = 3(A - 2) \tag{2}$$

Beth is eight years older than half as old as Craig will be

$$B = 8 + \tfrac{1}{2}(C + t_2) \tag{3}$$

when he is three years younger than Alex will be

$$C + t_2 = A + t_3 - 3 \tag{4}$$

when Beth will be twice as old as Alex will be seven years from now.

$$B + t_3 = 2(A + 7) \tag{5}$$

When Alex was two years old, Beth (who was $B - (A - 2)$ years old at that time) was four years older than Alex will be

$$B - (A - 2) = A + t_4 + 4$$
$$\rightarrow t_4 = B - 2A - 2 \tag{6}$$

when Craig will be one year younger than three times as old as Beth was

$$C + t_4 = 3(B + t_5) - 1 \tag{7}$$

seven years before the time

$$t_5 = t_6 - 7 \tag{8}$$

when Craig was half as old as Alex will be

$$C + t_6 = \tfrac{1}{2}(A + t_7) \tag{9}$$

when Beth will be 14 years older than she was

$B + t_7 = B + t_8 + 14$

$\rightarrow t_8 = t_7 - 14$ (10)

when Craig was one-sixth as old as a year more than Alex was

$C + t_8 = \frac{1}{6}(A + t_9 + 1)$ (11)

when Beth will be four times as old as she was when Craig was born. (Note: Beth was $B - C$ years old when Craig was born.)

$B + t_9 = 4(B - C)$

$\rightarrow t_9 = 3B - 4C$ (12)

Now that we have our equations, we need to do a good deal of substitution. Substituting for t_1 in equations (1) and (2), gives us:

$11A - 4B + 4C = 35$ (13)

Subbing for t_2 and t_3 in equations (3), (4) and (5), eventually gives us:

$B = A + 9$ (14)

Using equations (7) and (9) to sub for t_5 and t_6 in equation (8), gives us:

$t_4 = 3B - 4C + \frac{3}{2}A + \frac{3}{2}t_7 - 22$ (15)

And then using equation (6) to sub for t_4 gives us:

$t_7 = \frac{-7A - 4B + 8C + 40}{3}$ (16)

Subbing for t_9 in equations (11) and (12), and simplifying, gives us:

$t_8 = \frac{A + 3B - 10C + 1}{6}$ (17)

And then using equation (10) to sub for t_8, and simplifying, gives us:

$t_7 = \frac{A + 3B - 10C + 85}{6}$ (18)

Using equations (16) and (18), gives us:

$-15A - 11B + 26C = 5$ (19)

Now we have three equations (13), (14), (19) that are just in terms of the variables A, B and C.

Using equation (14) to sub for B in equations (13) and (19), gives us:

$7A + 4C = 71$

$-A + C = 4$

This readily gives us our final answer of:

$A = 5; B = 14; C = 9$

And, yes, we can also check our answer with the original problem statement to confirm that we are correct:

Eleven years from now Alex (age 16) will be four times as old as Craig (age 4) was when $(t_1 = -5)$ Beth (age 9) was three times as old as Alex was (age 3) two years ago. Beth (age 14) is eight years older than half as old as Craig (age 12) will be when $(t_2 = 3)$ Craig (age 12) is three years younger than Alex (age 15) will be when $(t_3 = 10)$ Beth (age 24) will be twice as old as Alex (age 12) will be seven years from now. When Alex was two years old, Beth (age 11) was four years older than Alex (age 7) will be when $(t_4 = 2)$ Craig (age 11) will be one year younger than three times as old as Beth (age 4) was $(t_5 = -10)$ seven years before the time when $(t_6 = -3)$ Craig (age 6) was half as old as Alex (age 12) will be when $(t_7 = 7)$ Beth (age 21) will be 14 years older than she (age 7) was when $(t_8 = -7)$ Craig (age 2) was one-sixth as old as a year more than Alex (age 11) was when $(t_9 = 6)$ Beth (age 20) will be four times as old as she (age 5) was when Craig (age 0) was born.

Now that was a bit crazy, wasn't it?

160. Dogs on a triangle

Let v be the speed of the dogs. We will focus now on the triangle, which is shrinking and rotating as the dogs are running. Looking at the triangle's base, we ask: What is the

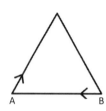

rate at which the length of the base is shrinking? If only dog B were running (horizontally to the left) then the base would be shrinking at a rate v, equal to the rate of the dog. However, dog A is also moving, and the horizontal component of its vector is $v\cos 60° = \frac{1}{2}v$. Therefore, the base of the triangle is shrinking at a rate of $1.5v$. Then, we can say that it takes $90 \div 1.5v = \frac{60}{v}$ seconds to shrink to a point. So the dogs run for a total distance of $v \times \frac{60}{v}$, which is 60 m.

Logic puzzles

161. Three men

The statement 'the bachelor and Lon have the same coloured eyes' tells us that Lon must be married and has brown eyes. Don is also married, so Ron must be the bachelor, and therefore must have brown eyes. So Don must have blue eyes, and Don has hair.

162. Saints and crooks

Assume that Bob is a crook. Then his statement would have to be true. But then he wouldn't be lying, so our assumption is wrong – he can't be a crook. Since Bob is a saint, what he says must be true. Therefore, Bill is a crook.

163. Labelling boxes

The strategy is to select (for your one clue) the box that is (incorrectly) labelled as 'one apple and one mango'. For example, imagine that you are shown an apple from that box. This tells you that that box should be labelled 'two apples'. It then follows that the box which was initially labelled as 'two mangos' should instead be labelled 'one apple and one mango', and the remaining box (which was initially incorrectly labelled 'two apples') should instead be labelled 'two mangos'.

164. Dominoes on a chessboard

The squares on a chessboard alternate between black and white. The two squares that were removed were both black. Each domino must cover one white square and one black square. After 30 dominoes have been placed, there must be two white squares left to be covered. Therefore, it is impossible to cover all of the squares with the 31 dominoes.

165. Two sisters

Numbering the facts as:

(1): The taller of Ann and Christy is the younger sister.

(2): The shorter of Ann and Betty is the older sister.

(3): The younger of Betty and Christy is the shorter sister.

Now we will consider the possibilities:

Possibility (1) Betty and Christy are the sisters:

If Betty and Christy are indeed the sisters, then fact (1) and fact (2) tell us that the order of their heights (from shortest to tallest) is

Betty, Ann, Christy, and that Betty must be older than Christy. But then, fact (3) wouldn't work. Therefore, Betty and Christy cannot be the sisters.

Possibility (2) Ann and Christy are the sisters:

If Ann and Christy are indeed the sisters, then fact (2) and fact (3) tell us that the order of their heights (from shortest to tallest) is Christy, Ann, Betty, and that Christy is the youngest of the three girls. But then, fact No. 1 wouldn't work. Therefore, Ann and Christy cannot be the sisters.

Possibility (3) Ann and Betty are the sisters:

If Ann and Betty are indeed the sisters, then fact (1) and fact (3) tell us that Ann is the tallest of the three girls, and that the order of their ages (from youngest to oldest) is Ann, Betty, Christy. Then fact (2) would work. Therefore, Ann and Betty are the sisters.

166. Five hats

The key to this problem is to seek out the contradictions and let them make the determination for you. This can be solved by the process of elimination, but you need a place to start.

Boy *B* could not see 4 red hats, because that would make all the other boys truth-tellers, but their statements contradict this. So Boy *B* is lying and has a yellow hat.

Boy *C* cannot be telling the truth. For if he were, then Boy *E* would also have to be telling the truth (since we already have determined that Boy *B* has a yellow hat), but then Boy *E*'s statement wouldn't work. So Boy *C* is lying and has a yellow hat.

If Boy *E* were telling the truth, then Boy *A* would be seeing three yellow hats and a red hat, but that would mean Boy *A* would also be telling the truth, which is a contradiction. So Boy *E* is lying and has a yellow hat.

Now we need only to determine the colour of the hats for Boy *A* and Boy *D*. They can't both be yellow, because that would make Boy *E* a truth-teller. The only thing that works is if Boy *A* and Boy *D* both have red hats.

Thus: *A* – red; *B* – yellow; *C* – yellow; *D* – red; *E* – yellow.

Lastly, we can confirm that this solution works by checking that all of the statements are consistent with the boys' hat colours.

167. The wizard and the old man

If the statement, 'I will give you my son' were true, then he would have to give up his daughter, so the statement would be false. If the statement, 'I will give you my son' were false, then he would have to give up his son, so the statement would be true. Therefore, it is not possible to say whether the statement is true or false, so he doesn't have to give up either his son or daughter.

168. The two-door riddle

The question Ben should ask one of the guards is, 'If I ask the other guard which door will lead to my freedom, what will he say?' No matter which guard he asks, the answer given will be the wrong door, so he should open the other door.

169. A and X

It is helpful to reframe the question, and instead ask ourselves, 'Which circles can't be filled in with an *X*?' We can then see that only the bottom-left circle can't be assigned an *X*, for that would lead to having one row with three *X*'s or three *A*'s.

170. Stolen chocolate

Mary and Larry contradict each other, so one of them must be telling the truth, and the other must be lying. Since we know that at least two are lying, then Jerry must be lying. So Jerry stole the chocolate.

171. Three suitors

If the first suitor had seen two yellow silks on the backs of the other two suitors, then he would have known that his silk had to be green, and he wouldn't have been wrong. Because he was wrong, this told the next two suitors that one or both of them must have had a green silk. The second suitor (who knew that either he or the last suitor must have a green silk) hoped he would see a yellow silk on the back of the last suitor – then he would have known for sure that his own silk was definitely green. But since he had to resort to guessing (and guessed wrong) he couldn't have seen a yellow silk on the third suitor. This is how the third suitor knew his silk had to be green.

Brain teasers

172. A very large hotel

Note: August has 31 days.
a) 2^{30} = 1,073,741,824.
b) It became half full on August 30.

173. Buckets

Perhaps the easiest way is to start by filling up the large bucket. Then you pour water from the large bucket into the small one, until the small bucket is full, and then discard the contents of the small bucket. Do this a total of three times, and you will be left with one litre in the large bucket.

   Another possible solution is to pour water from the small bucket into the large bucket. Each time, the small bucket needs to be filled completely, and once the large bucket is full, the water should be discarded from the large bucket, which should leave two litres in the small bucket. Pour that into the large bucket and then do it two more times, so you get 8 litres in the large bucket. Then you simply fill the small bucket, and pour into the large bucket until it is full. There is now one litre left in the small bucket.

174. Four people crossing a bridge

The key is to get the slowest people (Bob and Mary) to cross together and not have either of them cross back. Therefore, they cannot be the first pair across, and they cannot be the last pair across either (otherwise one of them would have had to bring the flashlight back across).

   The solution is then as follows: Abe and

Kate (the fastest people) cross first. Abe (but it could also be Kate) comes back across with the flashlight. Abe gives the flashlight to Bob and Mary who then cross over the bridge. They give the flashlight to Kate, who brings it back across the bridge. It all ends with Abe and Kate coming across together.

The total time taken is 17 minutes.

175. Two hourglasses

We first need to prepare for the 9-minute interval. To do this, we begin by starting both hourglasses at the same time. Once the 4-minute hourglass runs out, we immediately flip it. Once the 7-minute hourglass runs out, we stop the 4-minute hourglass (which has 1-minute's worth of sand left in it) by putting it on its side. We are now prepared for the 9-minute interval. To begin the 9-minute interval, we restart the 4-minute hourglass, which will finish in one minute. After it finishes, we complete the 9-minute interval by simply running the 4-minute hourglass two more times. (There are other possible solutions, as well.)

176. Fish bowl

100 goldfish need to be removed.

177. Stick puzzles

a)

b) The dark sticks are the ones that have been moved.

c)

d) Two solutions.

e)

f)

178. Ages of teenagers

There are five teenagers in the group, aged 18, 14, 13 and two are 15.

179. Magic cubes

a) The average of the numbers 1 to 8 is 4½. Therefore, the sum of each face must be 4 × 4½ = 18. The 8 is placed diametrically opposite from the 7, but on the same edge as the 1. The 2 is placed diametrically opposite from the 1. Filling in the rest of the cube leads to the solution shown here.

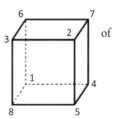

b) A key realisation is that no odd number can be connected to another odd number. Also 0 and 1 cannot be connected, because 1 is not prime. Here is one solution.

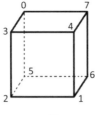

c) This one requires more experimentation. Here is one solution.

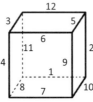

180. A long rope

At first glance, it may seem that this extra 100 m would somehow be spread out across the whole equator, and therefore the rope would barely be above the ground. But this is not the case. Whether the rope is going around the equator of the earth, the moon, or Jupiter doesn't matter; either way (as long as it is 100 m longer than that equator) it will be the same height above the ground.

If we increase the length of a circle's radius by x, then its circumference increases by $2\pi x$. Instead, if we increase a circle's circumference by x, then its radius increases by $x \div 2\pi$.

With the problem at hand, we can say that if a circle's circumference increases by 100, then its radius increases by $100 \div 2\pi \approx 15.9$. Therefore, the rope going around the equator will be about 16 metres high – far too high for any horse to jump over.

181. Equal products

The product of each of the three strings of digits must be equal, so the product of their prime factorisations must also be equal. Clearly, we can't use a 0. We also can't use a 5 or a 7, because if we did, then a 5 or 7 would have to appear in the other two prime factorisations, and that's not possible. Now let's consider the factor 3. The digit 9 contains two 3s (in its prime factorisation) and the digits 3 and 6 each contain one 3. Therefore, we will place the 9 at an intersect point, and the 3 and 6 on corners away from the 9. Now let's consider the factor 2. The digit 8 contains three 2s, the digit 4 contains two 2s, and the digits 2 and 6 each contain one 2. We simply think of this as we fill in the remaining places of the puzzle. The final answer is shown here.

8		3
9	2	4
1		6

182. A square and a triangle

There are infinitely many possible solutions for both of these.

a) Choose any number (5 or over) for the top circle. The bottom-left circle must then be 3 greater than the top circle, and the bottom-right circle must be 4 less than the top circle.

b) In this case, the key is to make it so that the two circles falling on the vertical midline (shown here as 23 and 3) have the same sum as the two circles falling on the horizontal midline (shown here as 10 and 16).

183. Pentagram and hexagram

a)

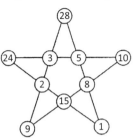

b)

One possible solution:

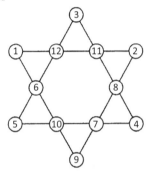

184. Magic star

Here, the points of the star can all be increased or decreased by the same amount, and the whole thing will still work.

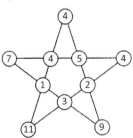

185. Connect-the-dot triangles

One systematic approach is to find all of the triangles that have a certain length side, and then move to another length side, being careful not to list one that is congruent to another previously listed triangle.

Using this method, we get the following.

9 triangles have a side length = 1: *ABF, ABG, ABH, ABJ, ABK, ABL, ABN, ABO, ABP*

8 triangles have a side length = 2: *ACF, ACH, ACJ, ACK, ACL, ACN, ACO, ACP* (not *ACG* because it is congruent to *ABJ*, listed above)

4 triangles have a side length = 3: *ADG, ADK, ADO, ADP*

3 triangles have a side length = $\sqrt{2}$: *EBK, EBL, EBP*

2 triangles have a side length = $\sqrt{5}$: *ECL, ECP*

1 triangle has a side length = $\sqrt{8}$: *ICP*

Therefore, there are a total of 27 non-congruent triangles.

186. The chess king

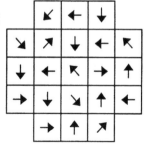

187. The three lights

Call the switches *A*, *B*, *C*. Turn on switch *A* and switch *B*. After 5 minutes, turn off switch *B*, and then walk into the room. Quickly feel the two light bulbs that are off; the warm one is controlled by switch *B*, and the other lamp that is off, is controlled by switch *C*. The lamp that is on is controlled by switch *A*.

188. Crossing a desert

a) There are many strategies that will get you 800 miles on four fill-ups. Here is one:

Trip 1: Drive 100 miles into the desert and drop off 300 miles of fuel. Return to start.

Trip 2: Drive 100 miles into the desert. Pick up 100 miles of fuel. Drive to mile 200. Drop off 200 miles of fuel. Return to start.

Trip 3: Drive 100 miles into the desert. Pick up 100 miles of fuel. Drive to mile 200. Pick up 100 miles of fuel. Drive to mile 300. Drop off 100 miles of fuel. Return to start.

Trip 4: Drive straight through, picking up 100 miles of fuel at mile 100, 200, and 300.

b) With an infinite supply of fuel, infinite supply of gas cans, and an infinite amount of time, any finite desert could be crossed.

189. Blood test

Out of a population of 100,000, the statistical average will be that one person will have the disease and, of the 99,999 that don't have the disease, 2000 (roughly) of them will falsely test positively for it. Since Jeff tested positive for the disease, there is a 1 in 2000 chance, or a 0.05% probability that he actually has the disease. (This seems to say that such a test would be a preliminary test, and that someone who tests positive should take an additional, more accurate test.)

190. Tiling a courtyard

This problem is harder than it appears at first glance.

First, we can determine the size of a single tile. If x is the length of the original tile's edge, then we get $1440x^2 = 1210(x + 2)^2$. Solving this results in $x = 22$. So the smaller tiles have 22 cm edges, and the larger tiles have 24 cm edges.

Proceeding further, we know that for the first tiling $L_1 \times W_1 = 1440$, where L_1 is the number of tiles running along the length of the courtyard, and W_1 is the number of tiles running along the width of the courtyard. For the second tiling $L_2 \times W_2 = 1210$, where L_2 is the number of tiles running along the length of the courtyard, and W_2 is the number of tiles running along the width of the courtyard. And since the length of the larger tiles is $^{12}/_{11}$ as long as the smaller tiles, we know that:

$L_2 = {}^{11}/_{12} L_1$ and $W_2 = {}^{11}/_{12} W_1$.

This tells us something helpful: L_1 and W_1 must multiply together to become 1440, and they must both be evenly divisible by 12. There are then only two possibilities for L_1 and W_1: 60 and 24, or 120 and 12. This means L_2 and W_2 must be either 55 and 22, or 110 and 11. Finally, we can say that the dimensions of the courtyard could be 1320 × 528 cm or 2640 × 264 cm. In metres, this is 13.20 × 5.28 m, or 26.4 × 2.64 m.

191. All triangles are isosceles?

The error is in the drawing. If constructed properly, the point E would be outside of the triangle. Because of the incorrect location of point E, the rest of the proof is thrown off.

192. A square from nowhere

The assumption that most people make is that the outline of the top and bottom figures are both right triangles. In fact, neither of them are even proper triangles, because the sloped line in the top figure is slightly dented inward, and the sloped line in the bottom figure is slightly dented outward. This is due to the fact that

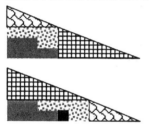

the two right triangles (within the figure) are not exactly similar – one has a base to height ratio of 5:2, and the other is 8:3.

193. The prisoners' dilemma

After developing several, seemingly clever strategies, it often shocks people to learn that you can save all but one prisoner!

Of course, the first prisoner (the one at the end of the line) cannot be helped; he has a 50% chance of being freed no matter what. This first prisoner has to use a binary code (by saying 'red' or 'blue') to indicate something useful. The rest of the prisoners then have to be able to use this information, combined with what he can see and hear, to determine his own hat colour.

The most useful piece of information (i.e.,

the 'binary code'), which the first prisoner can convey to the rest, is whether he sees an odd or even number of a particular hat colour in front of him. Then, as each prisoner goes, each remaining prisoner can keep track of the colours of the hats of the prisoners that have gone already, and also note the colours of the hats in front of him, in order to determine, with certainty, the colour of the hat that he himself is wearing.

The following example should clarify things. Assume the prisoners have agreed that the first prisoner should say 'red' if he sees an odd number of red hats, and 'blue' if he sees an even number of red hats. The big morning arrives, and they get into line. Now, imagine, that the first prisoner looks at the other prisoners' hats and says 'red' (indicating that he sees an odd number of red hats). And it turns out that he is lucky, so it is announced that he has correctly stated his own hat colour and thereby is allowed to go free. The rest of the prisoners now know that, altogether, there is an even number of red hats. Therefore, if the second prisoner sees an odd number of red hats in front of him, and he knows that the prisoner behind him had a red hat, then he knows that his own hat must be blue (in order to make the total number of red hats an even number). Likewise, each prisoner, when his turn comes, knows the colour of everyone else's hat (the ones that have already had their turn, as well as the hats he can see before him), and knows that there are an even number of red hats altogether (because of what the first prisoner indicated by saying 'red'), so he can thereby determine the colour of his own hat.

194. The three daughters

Because knowing her own age wasn't enough information, we know that there must be two sets of (three) numbers that both multiply to 72 and add to whatever the girl's age is. If we then list all the sets of three numbers whose product is 72 (e.g., 1, 1, 72 and 1, 2, 36, etc.) then we will find that only the following two sets have the same sum: 2, 6, 6 and 3, 3, 8. Most notably, each set shows that two of the three daughters are, in fact, twins. Therefore, when the man speaks of his 'oldest daughter', the girl can then conclude that 2, 6, 6 aren't the ages because, if that were so, there wouldn't be an 'oldest' daughter. So the answer must be that the daughters are 3, 3 and 8.

195. Weighing coins

a) Break the 12 coins into four groups of three. Compare the weights of group 1 and 2, and then group 3 and 4. You now know which of these groups has the lighter coin. Simply take two of the three coins from this group and weigh them. The lighter coin is either in this weighing, or, if these two coins are equal, the third coin is the lighter one. (Another solution can be arrived at by breaking the coins into three groups of four.)

b) The solution to this problem is all about contingencies – what is to be done at each weighing (after the first) depends on what happened before.

Divide the coins into three groups of four coins. For the first weighing, compare group 1 and group 2 on the balance scale, with group 3 set aside.

If groups 1 and 2 are equal, then you know the fake is in group 3. In this case, for the second weighing, take any two coins from group 3, and compare them against any two coins from the other groups (which you know to be real).

If this second weighing is equal, then you know the fake is one of the other two coins from group 3. So for the third weighing, we need to determine which of these two coins is the fake by doing the following:

In order to determine which of two coins (*X* and *Y*) is the fake, we compare coin *X* with another coin that we know is real. If these balance, then we know that *Y* is the fake; if they don't balance, then we know that *X* is the fake. (*)

If this second weighing is not equal, you know the fake is one of the two coins on the scale from group 3. So for the third weighing, we need to determine which of these two coins is the fake by following (*) above.

If groups 1 and 2 are not equal, you know the fake is one of the coins in group 1 or group 2, and things are a bit more complicated.

You'll find that the methods above won't find the fake out of the remaining eight coins in two weighings, so we need to get more information. For starters, we label the scale's heavier pan as *A*, and the lighter pan as *B*. At this point, we can say that either the fake coin is heavier and in pan *A*, or it is lighter and in pan *B*. Also, the four coins not on the scale (group 3) are all real coins.

For the second weighing, take three of the four coins from pan *A* and put them aside, move three of the four coins from pan *B* over to pan *A*, and, lastly, place three of the coins from group

3 into pan B. All of the above should be done while keeping an eye on the two coins in the pans that never moved. After doing all of this, there are now three possibilities.

Pan A remains heavier. Then the fake is one of the two coins we didn't move. In that case, for the third weighing, we need to determine which of these two coins are the fake by following (*) above.

Pan B becomes heavier. Then we know the fake is one of the three coins that were moved from pan B to pan A, and we know that the fake is lighter. So for the third weighing, we compare any two of these three coins. If they balance, then the last of the three is the fake; if unbalanced, the fake is the lighter of the two.

Pan A and pan B are equal. Then we know the fake is one of the three coins that were moved from pan A and put aside, and we know that the fake is heavier. So for the third weighing, we compare any two of these three coins. If they balance, then the last of the three is the fake; if unbalanced, the fake is the heavier of the two.

196. A hidden card

First of all, notice that, given any five cards, at least two of them must be the same suit. Thus we can use the first position to indicate the suit of the hidden card by placing in that position, one of the two cards that share a suit.

But the question is: which of these two same-suit cards do we put in the first position, and which should be chosen as the hidden card? To answer this, we first need to realise that there are only 13 cards in any suit, and that we want to determine the shortest route to count up from

one of these cards to the other. For example, if we have a 2 and a 10 of hearts, then it takes 8 steps to go from 2 up to 10, but only 5 steps to go from the 10 up to the 2 (i.e., 10, J, Q, K, A, 2). Our strategy will therefore be to make the 2 of hearts the hidden card, and put the 10 of hearts face up in the first position (labelled 1). Our partner will therefore know, at a quick glance, that the value of the hidden card is simply 5 steps up from the 10 of hearts. So now the question is: how could the placement of the other three cards indicate the number of steps to take?

To answer this last question, we only need to determine a way to have the first three cards indicate the numbers 1 though 6. Fortunately, there are 6 ways to arrange these three cards.

We can rank these last three cards in comparison to one another and thereby assign them each a value of 1, 2, or 3, where the highest is given a ranking of 3, and the lowest gets a 1. (In the event of a tie, the order of the suits is given, as in bridge, ♠ ♥ ♦ ♣.) We simply need to place them in a special order that indicates to our partner, through an agreed-upon special code, a number one through six. One possible scheme would be:

```
3, 2, 1 = 6        2, 1, 3 = 3
3, 1, 2 = 5        1, 3, 2 = 2
2, 3, 1 = 4        1, 2, 3 = 1
```

We now have a complete strategy. The card in the first position tells our partner the suit of the hidden card, and the remaining three cards indicate how many steps to go from the card in the first position in order to get to the hidden card.

Example: Imagine you are the partner. You walk into the room (after the cards have been dealt and placed upon the table) and see the cards in this order: 7♠, Q♦, 3♣, Q♥. You immediately know that you need to take a certain number of steps up from the 7♠. The ranking of the last three cards is 2-1-3, which, according to the above code, represents a 3. Therefore, going from 7♠ up by three steps, tells us that the hidden card must be a 10♠.

Note: The insight that there are only 13 ordered numbers to identify is called modular arithmetic, or 'clock maths'. In modular arithmetic, the numbers 'wrap' around after the modulus. On a clock, there are 12 numbers, so it is mod 12. We can say, for example, that '15 o'clock' is equal to 3 o'clock. In the cards, we are mod 13. Also, the ranking and coding of the card values is a clever combination of permutations and a sort of binary counting.

197. Money and a circle

Let n be the number of people, and x be the amount of money the poorest person had at the start. Then the richest man had $x + n - 1$ at the start (since he is $n - 1$ steps away from the poor person).

With each cycle around the circle, each person's money is reduced by £1. Therefore, after c cycles, the richest person has

$$x + n - 1 - c \qquad (1)$$

Clearly, the thing will end when the poorest person cannot give one more than he received. Therefore, it is going to be the (originally) poorest person who ends up with 4 times as much as the (originally) richest person. This will

have to be one cycle after the poorest person reached zero (which will happen after x cycles). This means $c = x + 1$. (Note that once the game has ended, everyone has passed the pot c times, except for the last, originally poorest, person. He didn't pass it the last time; instead he kept the whole pot.)

By subbing in $c = x + 1$ into (1) above, we can now say the (originally) richest person ends up with $x + n - 1 - (x + 1)$, which simplifies to $n - 2$.

Every time a cycle is completed, the pot increases by n. If c is the total number of cycles, then when the pot gets passed for the very last time, to the last (originally poorest) person, it will have $n \times c - 1$ pounds in it. By subbing in $c = x + 1$, we can say that the (originally) poorest person ends up with $n(x + 1) - 1$. And we know that this amount must be four times greater than what the (originally) richest person ended up with, which is $n - 2$ (as explained above). This gives us an equation to solve:

$$n(x + 1) - 1 = 4(n - 2)$$
$$nx + n - 1 = 4n - 8$$
$$nx = 3n - 7$$
$$x = 3 - \tfrac{7}{n}$$

This can only give a non-trivial (i.e., $n \neq 1$) integer solution if $n \leq 7$ and n is an integer factor of 7. Therefore, $n = 7$, and $x = 2$.

There were 7 people in the circle, and the poorest person started with £2.

198. Careful handshaking

You have three handshakings and two gloves. The first guest puts both gloves on his right hand and shakes hands with the president. The outside of the inner glove and inside of the outer glove remain untouched by any hand. The second guest shakes hands with the president using just the first guest's outer glove (the president then touches the outside which only he has touched so far). The third guest shakes hands with the president using the first guest's inner glove, but turned inside out, and then places it inside the second guest's glove. This way no person ever touched another, nor a part of a glove already touched by another.

Problem-solving exercises

199. Rolling a one

First of all, we should note that the objective is to determine the best strategy in order to maximise our average score per game. You are not trying to beat your classmates. Imagine you are playing alone.

There are 36 equally likely rolls for the two dice. Of these 36 possibilities, 11 of them contain a 1. The probability of getting a 1 is therefore $^{11}/_{36}$, and the probability of *not* getting a 1 is $^{25}/_{36}$. When a 1 isn't rolled, the average roll is an 8. If a 1 is rolled, the larger your score is (before the 1 was rolled), the greater your loss will be.

The expected (that is, average) increase (E) in your score, if you decide to stay standing, is equal to the expected increase (C) in your score when a 1 isn't rolled, *minus* the expected decrease (D) in your score when a 1 is rolled. Taking each of these two possibilities.

The expected increase (C) in your score when a 1 *isn't* rolled, is the average increase

when a 1 isn't rolled (which is 8) times the probability of not rolling a 1 (which is $^{25}/_{36}$). Thus, $C = 8 \times (^{25}/_{36})$.

The expected decrease (D) in your score when a 1 *is* rolled, is whatever your score was (x) just before the 1 was rolled, times the probability of rolling a 1 (which is $^{11}/_{36}$). Thus, $D = x \times (^{11}/_{36})$.

In summary:

$E = C - D \longrightarrow E = 8 \times (^{25}/_{36}) - x \times (^{11}/_{36})$

How is this formula useful? Well before your first roll, x is zero, so you expect your score to *increase* by $8 \times (^{25}/_{36}) \approx 5.55$. At some later point in the game, if you happen to have a score of 10 (and decide to stay standing), then you can expect your score to *increase* by $8 \times (^{25}/_{36}) - 10 \times (^{11}/_{36}) = 2.5$, which means, on average, you will *gain* 2.5 points if you stay standing for the next roll. If instead you happen to have a score of 50, and you stay standing, then $E \approx -9.72$, which means that you should expect (on average) to *lose* 9.72 points.

We are interested in determining the value of x such that the expected increase of the score is zero, which is the boundary between a positive expected increase (that is, a gain) and a negative expected increase (a loss). Putting zero in for E in the above equation gives us $x \approx 18.2$.

Therefore, the best mathematical strategy is to remain standing whenever the score is 18 or below, and sit down once the score exceeds 18.

200. Monty's choice

This problem received national attention when it appeared in *Parade Magazine* in 1990, in Marilyn vos Savant's column, Ask Marilyn. Peter Taylor's book (with the problem he calls 'Car and Two Goats') includes a wonderful, and outrageous account of the various letters that it prompted.

After having a fair bit of debate, it's nice to have the students do a simulation of the game, as follows. In groups of three, one is the contestant, one is the game show host, and one rolls a die and a tosses coin. The die and coin is rolled so that Monty, but not the contestant, can see the result. This roll of the die determines which door has the car; a 1 or 2 represents door *A*, a 3 or 4 represents door *B*, and a 5 or 6 represents door *C*. The contestant then chooses a door. Monty looks at the die to see if the contestant guessed the door with the car behind it, or not. If the contestant guessed correctly, then Monty looks at the coin – heads means Monty 'opens' the higher of the two remaining doors, and tails means he 'opens' the lower of the two remaining doors. (With the simulation game, 'opening' door *B* simply means that Monty announces to the contestant, 'Door *B* has a goat behind it.') If the contestant didn't guess the door with the car, then Monty ignores the coin and simply 'opens' the remaining door with the goat.

Once Monty has shown a door with a goat behind it, Monty says to the contestant that he may now either switch to the other remaining door, or stick to the door he originally chose. Each group should do a simulation at least 10 times with the switching strategy and an equal number of times with the sticking strategy. Once all of the data has been collected for the whole class, it should become apparent that the switching strategy is best, yielding around a $2/3$ probability of winning.

Of course, now the discussion can turn to trying to explain why this is true. The explanation for the 'sticking' strategy is easier. In this case, the probability of success is clearly not affected by which door Monty first opens; therefore the probability of winning is $1/3$.

The explanation for the 'switching' strategy is trickier. One way to look at it is that the contestant wins every time with the 'switching' if, and only if, he initially didn't guess the correct door. Why is this so? Well, if the contestant chose the wrong door, then Monty will open the other wrong door, and then switching to the third, remaining door, is always a winner. In other words, the probability of winning with a switching strategy is the same as the probability that the initial choice of doors was wrong, which is clearly a probability of $2/3$.

201. Two ants

a) There are many possible paths, but only one shortest path. If the ant just walks along edges, the distance would be 9 ft. The shortest path, however, is best seen if we unfold the box and place it on a flat surface. There are many possible ways to unfold the box, depending on which edges we choose to cut. The drawing here shows one way to unfold and lay the box flat, such that the shortest path becomes obvious.

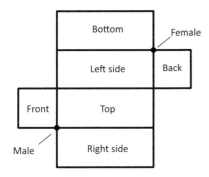

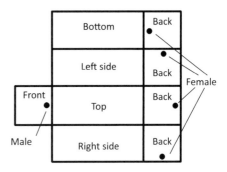

We now simply connect the two dots (the diametrically opposite corners of the box) to get the shortest path, which has a length of approximately 6.4 ft. Visualising this in three dimensions, this path takes the ant (which started at the top front right corner of the box) diagonally across the top and left side of the box. Of course, the same length path could have been achieved by walking diagonally across the right side and then the bottom of the box.

b) Following the above method, we first cut selected edges of the box, unfold it, and lay it out flat such that the male ant is seen closest to the top front edge of the box. The question then before us is: where is the best place to put the back face such that the shortest path becomes evident? The drawing (above right) shows the four possibilities for the placement of the back face – each placement of the back face yielding a different path by connecting the two ants with a straight line. The path that most people first think of takes the ant straight across the top face and has a

length of 7 ft (or 84 in). Next, consider the path that results from having the back face in the lowest position, or having the back face two squares from the top. Both of these paths have a length of approximately 81.4 in (calculated using the Pythagorean theorem). The shortest path of all, which has a length of exactly 80 in (or 6 ft 8 in), comes from placing the back face at the topmost square in the drawing. This path takes the ant across all but one of the faces of the box.

c) Given that the distance between two points is the shortest possible path between them, the two furthest points are the centres of the square faces, for a total length of exactly 7 ft.

d) I begin with the hypothesis that in order to be as far as possible from the male ant, the female must be on the opposite square face, fairly close to the corner that is diametrically opposite from the male ant. There are several paths possible that go from the male to the female, but clearly, in this case, any path that crosses three of the rectangular faces cannot be the shortest path. That leaves us with four possible paths that might be the shortest.

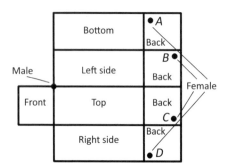

With the drawing here, the back square wall is shown in the four possible different foldouts, but the female ant is shown, in each case, in the same location. Connecting the female to the male with a straight line shows the four different paths.

If, for the moment, I only consider paths B and C, then I can see that as long as the female is somewhere along the diagonal line of the back square (the diagonal that passes through the right bottom back corner of the box) then paths B and C will have the same lengths. Likewise, at any point along this diagonal, paths A and D, will have the same lengths.

Now, imagining the female ant moving along this diagonal line, let's consider the lengths of paths A and B only. As it moves along this diagonal, the length of one of these two paths increases while the length of the other path decreases. The objective is to be at the location along this diagonal where the minimum path is the greatest. This location is where the lengths of these two paths (A and B) are equal. In fact, from this particular location, the lengths of all four of the paths (A, B, C and D) are equal. If

the female ant strays from this location, in any direction, then the length of at least one of the paths will decrease, and therefore the minimum path length is also decreased. Therefore, our goal is to find exactly where this location is such that the lengths of path and A and B are the same.

I assign x to the distance that the female is from the right back edge, and y to the distance that the female is up from the bottom back edge (the floor). (Note that with each back square in the drawing, these edges have been rotated.) The lengths are therefore:

Path A: $\sqrt{(4-x)^2+(y+5)^2}$

Path B: $\sqrt{(7-x)^2+(2-y)^2}$

Setting these equations equal, as well as setting x equal to y (since the location must be along the square's diagonal), yields: $x = y = \frac{3}{5}$, which means the female ant is located near the right bottom back corner of the box, 0.6 ft up from the floor and 0.6 ft away from the right wall. All four paths (A, B, C and **D**) from the male ant to the female at this location) have a length of 6.551 ft.

202. Lines and points
By looking at the initial example that starts with 4 lines drawn on the page, we can begin to analyse the problem and see some patterns.

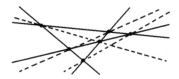

Starting with 4 lines.

The number of points of intersection is $_4C_2 = 6$.

Each line has 3 points on it.

Each point has 2 lines through it, and on these two lines there are a total of $2 \times 3 - 1 = 5$ points.

From each point, there is $6 - 5 = 1$ point to which a new line can be drawn.

The total number of new lines that can be drawn is $6 \times 1 \div 2 = 3$.

Starting with 5 lines.

The number of points of intersection is $_5C_2 = 10$.

Each line has 4 points on it.

Each point has 2 lines through it, and on these two lines there are a total of $2 \times 4 - 1 = 7$ points.

From each point, there are $10 - 7 = 3$ points to which a new line can be drawn.

The total number of new lines that can be drawn is $10 \times 3 \div 2 = 15$.

Starting with n lines.

The number of points of intersection is $_nC_2$.

Each line has $n - 1$ points on it.

Each point has 2 lines through it, and on these two lines there are a total of $2(n - 1) - 1 = 2n - 3$ points.

From each point, there are $_nC_2 - (2n - 3)$ points to which a new line can be drawn.

The total number of new lines is:
$$\tfrac{1}{2}\left[\,_nC_2(_nC_2 - 2n + 3)\right].$$

Here is a table of the results:

| n | | |
No. of starting lines	No. of pts intersection	No. of new lines
4	6	3
5	10	15
6	15	45
7	21	105
8	28	210
9	36	378
10	45	630

203. Cut plane

We will first solve a simpler version of the problem, and then see what insight it gives to the originally stated problem.

By reducing the number of planes, we can fairly easily visualise that 0 planes yield 1 region; 1 plane yields 2 regions; 2 planes yield 4 regions; and 3 planes yield 8 regions. One might be inclined at this point to see a pattern and conclude that the next step is 4 planes yield 16 regions, and therefore 10 planes will yield 1024 (2^{10}) regions.

| *Three dimensions* | |
planes	regions
0	1
1	2
2	4
3	8
4	15

However, on closer inspection, we start with the 8 regions that were produced by 3 planes and see that the fourth plane cuts through all but one of these 8 regions, thereby showing that 4 planes divide space into 15 regions. It is even more difficult to picture how many regions are produced by 5 planes. Certainly, trying to picture how many regions are created by 10 planes would be impossible.

The major insight is to simplify the number of dimensions of the original problem. Therefore, we ask: how many regions on a plane are produced by a certain number of lines? (Again, where all of the lines intersect with one another, but never three lines meeting at the same point.) This is quite manageable, and, as long as we are careful, we can progress quite quickly up to nine lines.

Two dimensions	
lines	regions
0	1
1	2
2	4
3	7
4	11
5	16
6	22
7	29
8	37
9	46

It usually doesn't take long before the students notice the pattern that generates this 2-dimension table. The differences in the 'regions' column keeps going up by one. And once that has been discovered, the students will likely discover two things:

1. The differences in the 3-dimension table (1, 2, 4, 7, etc.) appear to come from the 2-D table.

2. If we reduce from two dimensions to one dimension (that is, how many regions on a line are produced by a certain number of points?), then the resulting 'regions' column is simply the counting numbers (1, 2, 3, 4 ...). Quite nicely, we see that the differences in the 2-D table are given by the 1-D table, which seems to support our proposition stated in No. 1, above.

Of course, we can go ahead and fill out

the 3-D right away, but we are left with a bit of doubt as to whether proposition No. 1 (the differences in the 3-D table come from the 2-D table) is definitely true. How can we demonstrate that this is true?

Here is one possible approach. Let's start with the 2-D case of three lines (which divide the plane into 7 regions). The question is, how many additional regions are created by the fourth line?

To answer this question, we start by looking at the drawing on the right. We see that the new fourth  line intersects the other lines at 3 points. Each of the 4 segments that the 1-D line is broken into, corresponds to a new region on the 2-D plane.

In other words, our above 2-D question (how many additional regions are created by adding a fourth line?) can now be translated into this 1-D question, how many regions are produced by the 3 points of intersection on this new (fourth) line? The answer to both of these questions is 4, which can be found in the 1-D table, given opposite.

And in the same way, we can fill in the next place of the 3-D table by transforming this 3-D question – how many additional regions are created by the fifth plane? – into this 2-D question, how many regions are produced by the 4 lines of intersection on this new (fifth) plane? The answer to both questions (which is 11) can be found on the 2-D table. We now know 5 planes divide space into 15 + 11 = 26 regions.

One dimensions		Two dimensions		Three dimensions		Four dimensions	
points	regions	lines	regions	planes	regions	hyperplanes	regions
0	1	0	1	0	1	0	1
1	2	1	2	1	2	1	2
2	3	2	4	2	4	2	4
3	4	3	7	3	8	3	8
4	5	4	11	4	15	4	16
5	6	5	16	5	26	5	31
6	7	6	22	6	42	6	57
7	8	7	29	7	64	7	99
8	9	8	37	8	93	8	163
9	10	9	46	9	130	9	256
10	11	10	56	10	176	10	386

Now, we can fill out our tables, even past three dimensions.

Therefore, the answer to our original question is that 10 planes divide space into 176 regions.

Lastly, we leave with an interesting thought: what would all of this be in projective geometry? Answer: The number of regions would be found one row higher. For example, in 3-D projective space, 7 planes divide space into 42 regions.

204. The dartboard

a) $\left(\frac{11}{12}\right)^2 \times \frac{1}{12}$ —> ≈ 7.00%

b) Exactly 3 throws: $\left(\frac{11}{12}\right)^2 \times \frac{1}{12}$ —> ≈ 7.00%

Exactly 2 throws: $\left(\frac{11}{12}\right) \times \frac{1}{12}$ —> ≈ 7.64%

Exactly 1 throw: $\frac{1}{12}$ —> ≈ 8.33%

3 throws or less: Total ≈ 23.0%

c) Start with a simpler question: Imagine that someone hits the target 70% of the time on the first throw, 20% of the time on the second throw, and 10% of the time on the third throw (thereby never needing more than 3 throws). We then use weighted average to calculate the *expected* number of throws to hit the target:

$1(0.7) + 2(0.2) + 3(0.1)$ —> 1.4 throws.

However, with the given dartboard problem, the probability of hitting the target is $1/12$ (≈ 8.33%) for each throw. But, there is a chance (however small) that the target won't be hit until after several million attempts.

We can now create an infinite series where i is the number of throws needed to score, and $p(i)$ is the probability that we score on exactly that number of throws (and not earlier). The expected number of throws needed to score is again a weighted average, expressible as a series as follows:

$$\sum_{i=1}^{\infty} i\,[p(i)] \;\rightarrow\; \sum_{i=1}^{\infty} i\,[(\tfrac{11}{12})^{i-1} \times (\tfrac{1}{12})]$$
$$\rightarrow\; \frac{1}{12}\sum_{i=1}^{\infty} i\,(\tfrac{11}{12})^{i-1}$$

Now, there exists a particularly useful formula for this situation, which says:

$$\sum_{i=0}^{\infty} (i+1)x^i = \frac{1}{(1-x)^2}$$

but can also be written $\sum_{i=1}^{\infty}(i)x^{i-1} = \dfrac{1}{(1-x)^2}$.

Using this, we evaluate $\dfrac{1}{12}\sum_{i=1}^{\infty} i\,(\tfrac{11}{12})^{i-1}$ to get a result of 12.

Therefore, we expect to hit the target, on average, in 12 throws, which is what we may have suspected all along.

d) The Dartboard Principle states: *The expected (average) number of attempts needed to achieve a desired outcome is the reciprocal of the probability of getting the desired outcome in one attempt.*

205. Baseball cards

Let's start by asking a few simpler questions:

Question: What would be the expected (average) number of flips of a coin in order to get both possibilities (heads and tails)?

After one flip, you have one of the two possibilities – heads or tails. Since the chance of getting the other possibility on the next flip is $\tfrac{1}{2}$, the expected number of flips needed to get this other possibility will be 2. Therefore, the expected total number of flips is 3.

Question: What would be the expected (average) number of roles of a die, in order to get all six possible roles?

After one die has been rolled, the expected number of rolls needed to get a different result

is $\tfrac{6}{5}$, because the probability of getting it immediately is $\tfrac{5}{6}$ (again, this is the Dartboard Principle). Now we have achieved two different results in $1 + \tfrac{6}{5}$ rolls. The expected number of rolls needed to get a third different result is $\tfrac{6}{4}$, (because there is a $\tfrac{4}{6}$ probability of getting a different result in the next roll). Continuing this pattern, we see that the expected number of rolls to get all six results is:

$$\frac{6}{6} + \frac{6}{5} + \frac{6}{4} + \frac{6}{3} + \frac{6}{2} + \frac{6}{1} \;\rightarrow\; 6\sum_{i=1}^{6}\frac{1}{i} \;\rightarrow\; 14.7$$

Question: After having collected the 70th different baseball card (out of 200) what would be the expected (average) number of purchases needed in order to get another different card?

Again, using the Dartboard Principle, the probability that the next purchase will result in a different card is $\tfrac{130}{200}$. Therefore, the expected number of purchases needed in order to get a different card is $\tfrac{200}{130}$.

So now we return to the question at hand: What is the expected number of days needed to collect all 200 cards? Using what we have learned from the above questions, we get:

$$\frac{200}{200} + \frac{200}{199} + \frac{200}{198} + \ldots + \frac{200}{1} \;\rightarrow\; \sum_{i=1}^{200}\frac{200}{i}$$
$$\rightarrow\; 200\sum_{i=1}^{200}\frac{1}{i}$$

Unfortunately, the series $\sum\tfrac{1}{i}$ slowly diverges and has no easy formula associated with it. But by writing a simple computer program, we find that $\sum_{i=1}^{200}\frac{1}{i} \approx 5.878$, and therefore our final answer is that we expect it to take about 1176 days to collect all 200 cards.

206. Hitting ten

After some experimentation, it may be best to make some tables, where each table determines the probability of hitting N. We hope that we can build up to $N = 10$, and in the process see some pattern. With each table, we flip the coin as many times as needed, and state whether n was hit, or not. (Recall that heads is worth 1, and tails is worth 2. With the tables below, S = success, F = failure).

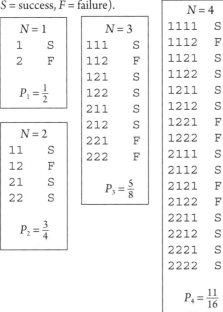

$N=1$	
1	S
2	F
$P_1 = \frac{1}{2}$	

$N=2$	
11	S
12	F
21	S
22	S
$P_2 = \frac{3}{4}$	

$N=3$	
111	S
112	F
121	S
122	S
211	S
212	S
221	F
222	F
$P_3 = \frac{5}{8}$	

$N=4$	
1111	S
1112	F
1121	S
1122	S
1211	S
1212	S
1221	F
1222	F
2111	S
2112	S
2121	F
2122	F
2211	S
2212	S
2221	S
2222	S
$P_4 = \frac{11}{16}$	

There are a few interesting patterns to notice. The top half of any given table is exactly the same as the entire previous table. (Can you explain why this is so?) The bottom half of each table has the same number of successes as the top half, except it's always one more or less, alternating. For example, with the $n = 3$ table,

the top half has 3 Ss, and the bottom half has one less (2 Ss), and with the $n = 4$ table, the top half has 5 Ss, and the bottom half has one more (6 Ss). Focusing now on the probabilities, the denominators are clearly powers of two. Each numerator is equal to twice the previous numerator, plus or minus 1. But the pattern that is perhaps most useful, is that each probability is just a slight adjustment from the previous table's probability. We simply take the previous probability and add or subtract 1 over the next power of two. For example,

$$P_3 = \frac{3}{4} - \frac{1}{8}, \text{ and } P_4 = \frac{5}{8} + \frac{1}{16}.$$

So the question now becomes: how can we find a general formula for P_n? Well, if we start from the beginning, we see that: $P_0 = 1$

$$P_1 = 1 - \tfrac{1}{2}$$
$$P_2 = 1 - \tfrac{1}{2} + \tfrac{1}{4}$$
$$P_3 = 1 - \tfrac{1}{2} + \tfrac{1}{4} - \tfrac{1}{8}$$
$$P_4 = 1 - \tfrac{1}{2} + \tfrac{1}{4} - \tfrac{1}{8} + \tfrac{1}{16}$$
$$P_n = 1 - \frac{1}{2} + \frac{1}{4} \dots \pm \frac{1}{2^n}$$

We can now recognise this as the general sum of a geometric series in the form $1 + x + x^2 + x^3 + \dots + x^n$, where $x = -\tfrac{1}{2}$. The general formula for this series is:

$$\sum_{i=0}^{\infty} x^i = \frac{x^{n-1} - 1}{x - 1}$$

Now plugging in $x = -\tfrac{1}{2}$ gives us
$$P_n = \tfrac{2}{3}\left[1 - \left(-\tfrac{1}{2}\right)^{n+1}\right]$$

This formula shows that as n becomes large, P_n approaches $\tfrac{2}{3}$. Since our goal is to determine the probability of hitting 10, we simply put 10 in for n and get $\tfrac{683}{1024}$, or 66.70% – very close to $\tfrac{2}{3}$ indeed.

207. Four sons

Of course, there are different methods for solving this problem. One possibility is recognising that we are working with a sequence of the form $x_n = a \times x_{n-1} + b$. In this case x_n is how much money the old man has after giving money to the nth son. We can then see that:

$x_n = \frac{3}{4}(x_{n-1} - 4) = \frac{3}{4} \times x_{n-1} - 3$ which then gives us:

$$x_1 = \frac{3}{4}x_0 - 3$$

$$x_2 = \frac{9}{16}x_0 - \frac{21}{4}$$

$$x_3 = \frac{27}{64}x_0 - \frac{111}{16}$$

$$x_4 = \frac{81}{256}x_0 - \frac{525}{16}, \text{ which is also}$$

$$x_4 = \frac{81x_0 - 2100}{256} \text{ where } x_0 \text{ is the original}$$

number of coins, and x_4 is the number of coins after giving coins to the fourth son.

So now the question is: what is the smallest positive integer that can be put into x_0 such that it will yield an answer for x_4 that is also a positive integer?

Writing a simple computer program can show that the first integral answer to this Diophantine equation is $x_0 = 244$ (and $x_4 = 69$).

208. Secret Santa

This problem is certainly very interesting, and there are several different paths to solving it.

One approach is to start with just 1 person, create a table that builds up one person at a time, and then look for patterns. With the table below, P is the probability that no person draws his own name.

For 1 person, we get $P = 0$.

For 2 people, $P = \frac{1}{2} = 0.5$

For 3 people, $P = \frac{2}{6} \approx 0.3333$

For 4 people, $P = \frac{9}{24} = 0.375$

For 5 people, $P = \frac{44}{120} \approx 0.3667$

For 6 people, $P = \frac{265}{720} \approx 0.36806$

For 7 people, $P = \frac{1854}{5040} \approx 0.36786$

For 8 people, $P = \frac{14833}{40320} \approx 0.36788$

We notice a few things. Firstly, the answer converges very quickly. In fact, quite surprisingly, once we get past 5 people, the probability (that nobody draws his own name) remains unchanged to three significant digits. The denominators of P are $n!$ which might be expected because it is the number of ways of arranging n people. The pattern with the numerators is more tricky. If we call the nth numerator h_n then it turns out that:

$h_n = n \times h_{n-1} + (-1)^n$ and most interestingly, that

$$P_n = 1 - \frac{1}{1!} + \frac{1}{2!} - \frac{1}{3!} + \frac{1}{4!} - \frac{1}{5!} \cdots \pm \frac{1}{n!}$$

This problem is most famously known as the Hat-Check problem. Euler solved the problem and recognised that the solution (approximately 0.367879) approaches $\frac{1}{e}$, as the number of people (n) approaches infinity.

Peter Taylor refers to this same problem as the game of 'snap'. He offers a nice solution and a very thorough explanation at *http://mast.queensu.ca/~peter/inprocess/snap.pdf*.

Fun With Maths Puzzles, Games and More

209. Prime factorisation

a) The prime factorisation of 109,350 is $2 \times 3^7 \times 5^2$. Given that a square number must have all even exponents in its prime factorisation, we can see that we need one more 2 and one more 3. Therefore, the answer is 6.

b) First some background. If a number has the prime factorisation $2^9 \times 3^8 \times 5^6 \times 13^4$, then we only need to look at the exponents of the 2 and the 5, in order to conclude that the number ends in 6 zeroes. Likewise, if a number's prime factorisation is $2^7 \times 5^{13} \times 7^2 \times 11 \times 23^3$, then we know that that number must end in 7 zeroes.

Now, to address the question at hand. Let $n = 4273!$ We know that the number of 2s in the prime factorisation of n must be greater than the number of 5s (that is, the exponent of the 2 must be greater than the exponent of the 5). Therefore, we simply need to determine the number of 5s in the prime factorisation of 4273! We can systematically do this by asking ourselves the following questions: How many numbers between 1 and 4273 are

Divisible by 5? Answer: 854.
Divisible by 25 (which is 5^2)? Answer: 170.
Divisible by 125 (which is 5^3)? Answer: 34.
Divisible by 625 (which is 5^4)? Answer: 6.
Divisible by 3125 (which is 5^5)? Answer: 1.
With a little bit of thought, we can now conclude that the number of zeroes in n must be equal to the sum of the above answers, which is 1065.

c) Let $n = 9,489,150,000$. n's prime factorisation is $2^4 \times 3^5 \times 5^5 \times 11 \times 71$. To produce a factor of n, we can choose anywhere from 0 to 4 twos, 0 to 5 threes, 0 to 5 fives, 0 or 1 eleven, and 0 or 1 seventy-one. This is now the same kind of problem as the typical wardrobe problem (How many different outfits are possible if you have 2 pairs of shoes, 5 trousers, and 4 shirts to choose from? – there are 40 possible outfits). In the case of determining the number of factors of n, we have 5 choices of twos, 6 choices of threes, 6 choices of fives, 2 choices of elevens, and 2 choices of seventy-ones. Therefore, n has 720 factors.

For some of the problems below, the following theorem is helpful:

If a number Q has exactly n factors, where n is a prime number, then Q's prime factorisation must be in the form $Q = k^{(n-1)}$, where k is a prime number.

d) There are many possible solutions, including 12 or 20.

e) There are two possible variations for this: either k^9, where k is a prime number (for instance, $2^9 = 512$), or $k \times h^4$, where k and h are prime numbers (for instance, $11 \times 3^4 = 891$).

f) Since n is a prime number (see above theorem), our answer must be k^6, where k is a prime number (e.g., $2^6 = 64$).

g) There are two possible variations for this: either k^8, where k is a prime number (for instance, $5^8 = 390,625$), or $k^2 \times h^2$, where k and h are prime numbers (for instance, $2^2 \times 5^2 = 100$).

h) Since n is a prime number (see above theorem), our answer must be k^{12}, where k is a prime number, such as $2^{12} = 4096$.

i) There are two possible variations for this: either k^{14}, where k is prime numbers (for instance, $3^{14} = 4,782,969$), or $k^2 \times h^4$, where k and h are prime numbers (for instance, $5^2 \times 2^4 = 400$).

210. Angles in a star polygon

a) 180°

b) 540°

c) No, the results would be the same. One explanation is that each angle of the star polygon can be considered an inscribed angle, with each of these angles subtending an arc of the circle. With part *a*, each arc gets subtended once, and with part *b*, each arc is subtended three times – and it doesn't matter if the points are evenly spaced or not.

d) 180°

e) 1980°

f) $s = 180 \times (n - 2x)$

Further reading

Angiolino, Andrea, *Super Sharp Pencil & Paper Games,* Sterling Publishing, 2000.

Bell, R.C., *The Boardgame Book,* Marshall Cavendish, 1979.

Frohlichstein, Jack, *Mathematical Fun, Games and Puzzles,* Dover, 2011.

Joris, Walter, *100 Strategic Games for Pen and Paper,* Carlton Books, 2002.

Knizia, Reiner, *Dice Games Properly Explained,* Blue Terrier, 2010.

Parlett, David, *Oxford History of Board Games,* Echo Point Books, 2018.

Sackson, Sid, *A Gamut of Games,* Dover, 2015.

Tahan, Malba, *The Man Who Counted,* W.W. Norton, 2015. This is a wonderfully creative story about the adventures of a mathematician in ancient Arabia. The stories and maths problems are well-suited for Classes Six and higher.

York, Jamie, *A Student Workbook for Mathematics in Class 7,* Floris Books 2016.

—, *A Teacher's Source Book for Mathematics in Classes 6–8,* Floris Books 2016.

Peter Taylor has a collection of problems online at *www.mast.queensu.ca/~peter/inprocess/contents.htm.* This is a great resource for rich problems, and also includes many entertaining stories from the classroom.

Index

Numbers refer to the puzzle number, *not* to the page

(*Act*) Classroom activities
(*Alg*) Upper School algebraic puzzles
(*Cl 4*) Class 4 (etc.)
(*Game*) Games
(*Geom*) Upper School geometric puzzles

(*Logic*) Upper School logic puzzles
(*Prob*) Upper School problem solving exercises
(*Tease*) Upper School brain teasers
(*Trick*) Maths magic tricks

Fun With Maths Puzzles, Games and More

MAKING MATHS MEANINGFUL

Books for Students

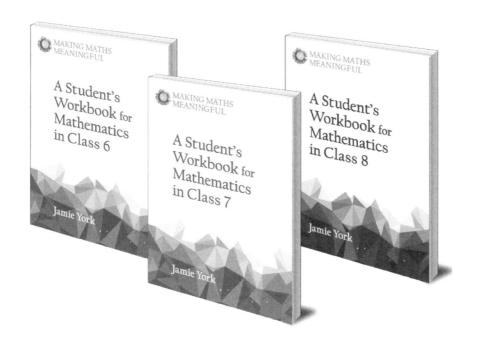

florisbooks.co.uk

Books for Teachers

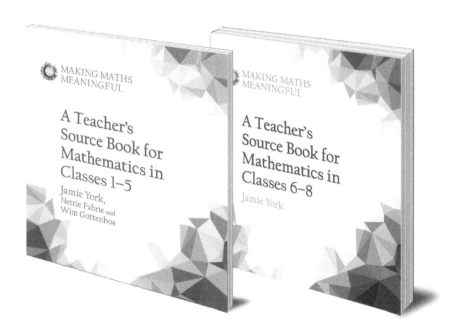

Jamie York's unique maths books are available for Classes 1 to 8, with two comprehensive teacher's source books plus separate student workbooks for Classes 6, 7 and 8. Workbooks are available individually or in classroom packs with a teacher's answer booklet, and have been fully revised for use in UK schools.

Floris Books

For news on all our **latest books,**
and to receive **exclusive discounts,**
join our mailing list at:

florisbooks.co.uk

Plus subscribers get a FREE book
with every online order!